The Wisdom of
the Poor One
of Assisi

The Wisdom of the Poor One of Assisi

by Eloi Leclerc

adapted from a translation by
Marie-Louise Johnson, M.D.

Hope Publishing House
Pasadena, California

Originally published in French under the title:
Sagesse d'un Pauvre.

Copyright © 1992 Hope Publishing House

Hope Publishing House
Southern California Ecumenical Council
696 South Madison Avenue
Pasadena, California 91106 - U.S.A.
Telephone: (818) 792-6123; FAX (818) 792-2121

Cover design - Christina Rodriguez

Cover icon - Kiko Argüello

Adapted from a translation by Marie-Louise Johnson, M.D.

Printed in the U.S.A. on recycled, acid-free paper.

Distributed by Spring Arbor Distributors

Library of Congress Cataloging-in-Publication Data

Leclerc, Eloi
    [Sagesse d'un pauvre. English]
    The wisdom of the poor one of Assisi / by Eloi Leclerc ;
adapted from a translation by Marie-Louise Johnson.
        p.   cm.
    Translation of : Sagesse d'un pauvre.
    ISBN 0-932727-47-6 -- ISBN 0-932727-45-X (pbk.)
    1. Francis, of Assisi, Saint, 1182-1226--Fiction. 2. Italy--
History--13th century--Fiction. I. Title.
PQ2672.E2154S2413 1992
843'.914--dc20   91-27207
                                            CIP

Contents

Preface

The most awesome sentence which has been pronounced against our times may well be this: We have lost our innocence. To say that does not condemn the progress of science and the technical advances of which our world is so proud. Such progress is, in itself, admirable. However, we must recognize that the progress was not achieved without a significant loss on the human level. Priding ourselves on our science and our techniques, we have lost something of our candor.

We hasten to add that there was more than mere candor and innocence in our ancestors. Christianity had taken over the ancient and earthy wisdom of peasants—a wisdom born of contact with the soil. There was, no doubt, more earth than Christianity in the hearts of a fair number of our ancestors, more indolence than grace. But mighty roots existed and the impetus of faith, like human loyalty, rested on vital ties—instinctive and extremely powerful—which were neither shaken nor exhausted.

In losing this simplicity, we have also lost the secret of happiness. All our science and technology leave us disquieted and alone. Alone, facing death. Alone, facing our own inconstancy and that of others, lost in the vast human herd. Alone, we wrestle with devils who harass us. When suddenly we comprehend our condition, we realize there is nothing which can give us a joy-filled life unless we go back to draw from the original source—which also carries us back to our youth. The word of the Gospel has never seemed so weighted with human truth. "Unless you become like little children again, you shall not enter the Kingdom of Heaven" (Mt 18:3).

On the road which leads to the spirit of childhood, a person as guileless and peaceful as Saint Francis of Assisi has something to say to us, something essential and decisive. This saint of the Middle Ages is astonishingly near to us. He seems to have felt and understood our problems in advance. It was he who wrote, "Hail, Queen Wisdom, may God save thee with thy sister, pure Simplicity." Oh, we know it only too well; there can be no wisdom for us who are so rich in science unless we return to pure simplicity. Who then could teach us the meaning of pure simplicity better than the Poor One of Assisi?

It is the wisdom of Saint Francis that this small book intends to evoke: his soul, his basic attitude before God and humanity. We have not sought to write a biography but have aimed only at a true glimpse of him with a fidelity that is less literal, more introspective and more profound than that of a simple historical narrative. One may approach a life such as that of Saint Francis from the outside, beginning with actual facts, then seeking step-by-step to penetrate eventually the soul of the saint. This is the ordinary method, always necessary; but when one proceeds thus and succeeds in grasping something of the treasures within, one may then attempt to describe this bounty and make it discernible. At this point, perhaps, one ought to resort to a mode of expression more akin to art than to history proper lest one betray the richness perceived.

With this concern for fidelity, more spiritual than literal, we have set out to portray the Franciscan Experiment under its double aspect. On the one hand, the experience sparkles with sunshine and mercy. On the other, it thrusts itself into the darkness of utter privation. The two aspects are inseparable. The wisdom of the Poor One of Assisi, however spontaneous and radiant it may seem, did not escape the universal law—it was the fruit of experience and trial; it matured slowly in meditation and detachment which deepened with time.

The privation of the Poor One reached its height in the very grave crises which shook his order and which he felt himself in a very distressing manner. The following account attempts to express the profound attitude of Saint Francis all through this hard trial. The discovery of wisdom was inscribed for him in an experience of salvation, of rescue, stemming from a distressful situation: "Hail, Queen Wisdom, may God save thee. . . ." Francis understood that wisdom itself needs to be saved—that it can be only the wisdom of the saved.

The beginning of the crises to be described was evoked, as

everybody knows, by the very rapid development of the order and the massive entrance of clerics into the community of lay-brothers. This new situation posed a difficult problem of adaptation. The friars, numbering 6,000, could no longer live under the same conditions as when they were merely twelve. Furthermore, additional needs made themselves felt in the midst of the community because of the presence of many educated individuals. An adaptation of the original ideal to the new conditions of existence was necessary.

Saint Francis was keenly aware of this. But he realized, too, that among the friars demanding the adaptation, many were prompted by a spirit that was not his. No one understood better than he the originality of his ideal. He felt responsible for this form of life which the Lord himself had revealed to him in the Gospel. Above all, he felt compelled not to betray this first, divine inspiration. In addition, he wanted to avoid shocking the legitimate sensitivity of his first companions—those simple souls could not help being disturbed by rash innovations. The adaptation was proving, therefore, a delicate task. It required much discernment, tact and time. But these conditions were not respected. The vicars-general to whom Francis had entrusted the government of the order during his sojourn in the Near East displayed an imprudent alacrity and changes were rushed through. The result was a grave crisis which threatened to go as far as disruption.

This predicament was a terrible trial for Francis. He felt himself a failure. But God was there waiting for him: it was a supreme purification. With a shattered spirit, the Poor One of Assisi proceeded toward a complete and definitive renunciation of himself. Through misery and tears, he was at last to attain peace and joy. At the same time, he saved his own friars by disclosing to them that the most exalted form of evangelical poverty is also the most realistic: it is one in which one acknowledges and accepts reality, both human and divine—reality in all its dimensions. It was the way to salvation for his order; a way which did not isolate itself in a sort of Reformation before Luther, but found within the church itself an interior equilibrium and permanence.

—*Eloi Leclerc*

1

Where There Is No Longer Peace

Leaving the dusty road and the broiling sun under which they had trudged for hours, Brother Francis and Brother Leo followed a narrow path which led through the woods toward the mountain. They proceeded painfully for both were weary. Their heavy robes of brown sackcloth had been unbearably warm in the full sun and now—how they did welcome the shadows which fell from the beech trees and the oaks!

The narrow ravine rose sharply and their awareness of every step was intensified by the rough pebbles under their bare feet.

At one point where the slope became quite steep, Francis stopped and sighed. His companion, a few feet ahead, stopped, too, and turning toward him asked in a voice filled with respect and affection, "Shall we rest here for a moment, Father?"

"Yes, let us, Brother Leo," answered Francis.

The two friars sat down side by side at the edge of the path, their backs supported by the trunk of an enormous oak tree.

"You seem very tired, Father," observed Brother Leo.

"As a matter of fact, I am," said Francis. "And you are too, no doubt, but up there in the solitude of the mountain, things will be better. It was time for me to leave. I could no longer stay in the midst of my brothers."

Then Francis became silent; he closed his eyes and remained motionless, his hands clasped around his knees, his head tilted back a bit, leaning against the tree. Leo looked at him attentively and was alarmed by what he saw—a countenance not only hollowed and emaciated but ravaged and clouded by profound sadness.

In this face, once so radiant, there was not the least glimmer of light. Here was the shadow of distress, of an inner anguish that sent down its roots into the depths of the soul and strangled him slowly. One might have thought this the face of someone in the throes of a terrible agony. A deep furrow was gouged across his brow and his mouth was set bitterly.

Up above, hidden in the thick foliage of the oak, a turtledove sounded Francis' thoughts. He was constantly drawn back in spite of himself to Portiuncula—that humble bit of land near Assisi so dear to his heart, as dear as the small Church of Our Lady which he had restored with his own hands. Was it not there, 15 years ago, that the Lord had given him the grace to join with a few friars and live according to the Holy Gospel?

Then all was beautiful and luminous as an Umbrian* springtime. The friars formed a true community of friends. Among themselves their relationships were easy, simple, unclouded. Truly their life had the crystal clarity of springwater. Each was submissive to all and had only one desire—to follow the life and the poverty of the most exalted Lord Jesus Christ. And the Savior blessed this little band for it multiplied rapidly and small communities of friars sprouted up through all of Christendom.

Now, however, everything was in danger. Among the friars the unanimity and simplicity had come to an end. Some spoke critically; others tore each other apart. There were those eloquent and influential members recently admitted to the order who declared without wincing that the Rule, as it was, no longer answered the needs of the community. They had their own ideas in the matter.

It was necessary, they said, to organize this vast number of friars into an order of strong structure and hierarchy. For this they must be enlightened by the legislation of the great ancient orders and must not reject extensive and permanent possessions which would give

---

*   Region of central Italy crossed by the Tiber.

the Order of Friars Minor its own place on the map. In the church as everywhere, they added, one has the place one takes.

"These newer friars," mused Francis sadly, "do not have the taste for evangelical simplicity and poverty."

He saw them undermining the work that he had accomplished with the aid of the Lord and it pained him horribly. And then there were the others—those who, under the guise of evangelical freedom or even the attitude of self-deprecation, indulged in all sorts of fantasies and eccentricities in the worst possible taste. Their behavior disturbed the faithful and brought discredit on all the other friars. These, too, were undermining the work of the Lord.

Francis opened his eyes and stared in front of him, murmuring, "There are too many Friars Minor."

Then, abruptly, as if to chase away this troublesome idea, he stood up and went on his way.

"I long to get to that spot where I shall find a true nest of the Gospel," he said. "On the mountain, the air is purer and a person is closer to God."

"Our brothers Bernard, Rufino and Sylvester will be happy to see you again," said Leo.

"I, too, shall be pleased to see them once more," said Francis. "They have remained faithful to me; they are the companions of the early days."

Leo walked ahead. Francis followed painfully; he was thinking of the months that he had just spent at the convent of Portiuncula during which he had redoubled his efforts to bring his brothers back to their vocation. The last general chapter, held at Pentecost, had brought all the friars together in one place. Even though he had told them clearly what was on his mind, he quickly realized that he and an important faction of the community were no longer speaking the same language. To try to convince them was a waste of time. So he had stood up before his 3,000 assembled friars, proud and fierce as a mother stands against anyone who would tear away her children, and cried out, "The Gospel does not need to be justified. Take it or leave it."

His early disciples, the faithful companions, had rejoiced. They hoped that he was going to take charge of his order, but his physical strength betrayed him. Francis had returned from Palestine with his health completely broken. To face the malcontents, one had to be strong, with a leader's robust temperament. Cardinal Hugolin, protector of the order, had thus advised Brother Elias to take the leadership and Francis had acquiesced—although not without misgivings.

For his own part, suffering with ailments of the liver and stomach, his infected eyes burned by the sun of the Near East as well as by tears, Francis had kept to a course of silence and prayer. But a heavy sadness had descended upon him like a sort of blight; it clung to his soul and corroded it, never ceasing to gnaw at him by night and day. To him, the future of his order seemed gloomy indeed. He saw his own flock divided. Some even reported to him that certain friars were giving a bad example and scandalizing the faithful. Brother Elias himself, as the head of the order, was putting on the airs of a great lord and playing into the hands of the innovators.

Francis was so grieved he was unable to hide it. No longer could he face his brothers with an open, joyous countenance as had been his custom. That is why he was now withdrawing far from them to hide his grief in the mountains, in the midst of the woods. He had resolved to retire to one of the hermitages that he had founded himself a few years before on the lower mountains buttressing the Apennines. There at least, in silence and solitude, he would no longer hear talk of a friar's bad example. There too, he would fast and pray until the Lord took pity on him and deigned to show him his face.

When Francis and Leo reached the summit of the first hill, they saw before them the small mountain covered by woods which hid the humble hermitage of the friars. They stopped for a moment to contemplate this verdant pyramid thrust up in front of the lower Apennines. Dense foliage adorned this side of the slope, masking its rugged and wild character. The other side, which was hidden from view but which Francis knew well, was a much steeper, more precipitous mass of fallen rock.

Above the mountain and as far as the eye could see, the sky was wonderfully clear and brilliant. It was a beautiful and tranquil evening in late summer. The sun had just disappeared behind the crest of the high mountains. There was nothing left but a misty glow in the west and imperceptibly the air began to freshen. A thin bluish haze lifted from the crevices of the earth and floated here and there above the purple ravines.

The path now wound its way up the hillside and the two brothers followed it slowly, in silence. Francis walked a little stooped, his eyes fixed on the ground. He plodded along like someone who labored under a burden that was too heavy.

Francis was crushed not by the weight of years, for he was hardly more than 40, nor was it the weight of his sins, although he had never felt so great a sinner before God as he did now. Nor was it the weight of the order in general; he did not know the order in general. In fact, Francis knew nothing in a general manner.

Something far heavier than abstract views was needed to weigh him down. The load which staggered him was his concern for each one of his individual friars. Whenever he thought of his friars—and now he never stopped thinking of them—he could see each with his own individual physiognomy, each with his particular joys and sufferings which Francis had the gift of making his own.

He felt the drama that was now being played in the hearts of so many of his sons and he felt it with the nuances appropriate to each of them, in a manner profound and poignant, for he had an extraordinary power of empathy. It was really like a maternal instinct which, perhaps, he inherited from his mother, Donna Pica. "If a mother nourishes and cherishes her child according to the flesh," he loved to repeat, "how much more should we nourish and cherish our brothers according to the spirit!"

When he was still a young man and in the world, his exquisite sensitivity made him particularly receptive and vulnerable. It made him vibrate to all that was living, young, noble and beautiful: to knightly deeds, to the poems of courtly love, to the enchantment of nature, to the charms of friendship. But it was also this sensitivity which aroused his pity for the poor and shook his entire being when one of them would come to him begging something "for the love of God."

His conversion had not deadened this humanity but had in fact deepened and purified it. God had made him feel the futility of his life and Francis had trained himself to focus on more profound challenges. There was the leper whom he met one day in the countryside of Assisi and whom he kissed in spite of strong revulsion. There was the crucifix of the small church of San Damiano which had come to life before his eyes, bidding him, "Go, Francis, repair my house which, as you see, is falling into ruin." His power of feeling had thus deepened while it had assumed an ever greater capacity for suffering.

Now the day was drawing to a close. Under the elms and pines which sprawled over the rocks, it was already dark. From the woods came the hoot of the owl and Leo observed: "We shall not arrive before nightfall."

Francis said nothing, but he was thinking that it was better that way. The brothers at the hermitage would be less apt to notice his melancholy.

They walked past a small spring where the friars came for water each day—the murmur in the darkness signaling its presence. Now they knew they were not far from their goal—just a stone's throw or two.

Suddenly a question occurred to Francis. Whenever he entered a house, it was his custom to say, "Peace to this house," just as the Lord requested in the Holy Gospel. But did he still have the right to say it? Was it not deceptive on his part to offer something that he himself did not have, or to present himself as a messenger of peace when in his heart there was no peace?

Francis lifted his eyes to heaven. The black silhouettes of the pines loomed on either side of the path and between their branches stretched a narrow band of dark blue sky. One by one, the stars began to appear. He sighed. In his night there were no stars. Must he wait for daybreak in order to follow the Gospel and to submit to the request of the Lord?

At that moment they had reached the plateau of the small oratory of the hermitage. Brother Leo had already gone around to the back. Then Francis, lifting his voice, cried into the silence of the night:

"In the name of the Lord, peace to this house."

And the words echoed back: ". . . to this house."

2

Alone in the Night

Adjoining the small oratory was the brothers' house—if one could call it a house! It was a simple hut built of mud and covered with branches. Five or six persons were enough to fill it. A pitiful gleam of daylight entered through a narrow opening in the wall. The floor was bare rock and the only furniture a bench of stone and a large cross of black boxwood which hung on the wall. Some large stones in a corner formed a fireplace. The hut served as kitchen, dining hall and community room.

The friars did not live there, however, but in their cells which were not far away on the steep slope of the mountain. The cells were natural caves, hollowed deep in the rock, to which one gained access through the midst of fallen boulders. In order to reach these shadowy holes in the cliff, one had to be as agile and light-footed as a mountain goat—in some places actually scrambling from rock to rock as the trail wound above the steep ravine.

The coming of Francis and Leo to the hermitage did nothing to change the life of the friars. Things were exceedingly simple there on the heights and they followed the Rule which Francis himself had previously dictated for the hermitages.

"Those who wish to live the religious life at the hermitage," Francis had declared, "shall live there in groups of three or four at the most. Two shall be in charge of the material things and procure the necessary food for all. Let them be as mothers and consider the others as their children. They shall lead the life of Martha while the other two attend only to their prayers until that time when they exchange functions."

Thus, one pair of brothers after another took upon themselves the material maintenance of the small community while the others gave themselves freely to meditation. In this wild and treacherous mountain scene, where all moving about meant difficult climbing or rapid and dangerous descent, the body itself had to undergo a discipline of conformity and purification which made it more docile to the spirit. In order to live this contemplative life one needed the coordination of a tumbler or an acrobat. A friar could not fear creeping on hands and knees, nor wearing out clothes on the rough rocks.

These acrobatics, thought Francis, were a way of

praising God. This was also a bit of great wisdom: the body and soul, so intimately associated and sharing in the same upward climb, found themselves united and in true peace of mind.

Without comfort or glamour, this life did not permit any disguise. There one was compelled to face one's own true self. In keeping with the surroundings, the friars tended to become sparing in words and gestures. Feelings, too, were assuaged and became more simple—not by dint of reading or inner search, but through a holy and harsh obedience to those things which poverty demands when it is accepted in all its right. It was a hard school, but there a person learned a new way of perception—a way much more simple and more real.

The only books known at the hermitage were those of the Holy Liturgy, the Missal and the Book of Canonical Hours. There was only a single copy of these books for all the friars; however, the word of God contained in these books was rediscovered in all its meaning and, in a way, in its original vigor. It was neither devitalized nor disturbed by a host of other readings.

Furthermore, nothing aids the savoring and understanding of the word of salvation as much as living at the ascetic breaking point. It is only when one is exposed to inclement weather that one knows the meaning of a roof. So too, when one lives far from all human support, from all which habitually gives existence a semblance of solidity, only then can one test for oneself the truth of words such as these: "My rock, my fortress, it is you." At such a time, a person without fearing can see one's existence tremble like the frail stem of a columbine in the crevice of a rock above the steep ravine.

At the close of day, when the brothers were reunited in the small oratory and recited at Compline the verse, "Protect us, Lord, as the pupil of your eye," they know that they were expressing something vital. Then all of these oft-repeated prayers held for them the zest of the real thing. There was not God on one side and reality on the other. God was real, at the very heart of reality.

Francis had proven many times the benefit of this life of solitude. But this time, although several days had elapsed since his arrival at the hermitage, peace had not returned to his soul. In the early morning, he assisted at the Lord's Supper that Brother Leo celebrated. Then he withdrew into solitude and prayed at length. He was in the throes of great anguish.

It seemed to him that God was alienated from him and he wondered if he had not presumed on his own strength. During these moments, Francis had recourse to the Psalms to express his agony. "You have estranged my friends from me," he said to God. "I have become as a stranger among my brothers. My eyes are consumed in grief. I stretch out my hands toward you. Why do you reject my soul? Why do you hide your face from me? I am oppressed by terrors. I am racked with fear."

But his prayer grew more urgent when he recited this verse: "Show me your way, O God, O Eternal One." Into this supplication he poured his entire soul for he was expressing his overpowering desire to know the will of God for him. He no longer knew what God wanted of him and he asked himself in anguish what he must do to be acceptable to God.

Since his conversion Francis had not ceased to reach out toward the good. He thought he had submitted to God's direction—and yet he had found failure. In attempting to follow the poverty and humility of the Lord Jesus Christ he had thought only of peace and goodness. Yet under his feet weeds had sprouted up and had seeded everywhere.

Often his prayer was prolonged into the night. One evening while he was still at prayer a great thunderstorm struck. Night had already come—a night heavy and veiled but suddenly lit by flickering lightning. In the distance the thunder boomed with a dull, hollow sound. Little by little the rumblings drew closer and soon the thunderstorm burst in all its fury just above the hermitage. Each clap sounded like the enormous blow of a battering ram against the mountain.

At first, a sudden strident noise broke forth in the pinnacle of the heavens, like the sound of tearing cloth. Then there was a dreadful crack and the crash reverberated against the mountain. It seemed that whatever came falling from heaven continued its din under the earth in a roaring which made everything tremble.

Alone in the night, Francis, too, was trembling—but not from the fear that terrifies people when they feel their life threatened. He was trembling because he did not know the plan of God for him. He asked himself what God wished of him and he feared that he might not hear God's voice.

This evening, the voice of God was in the storm. But one had to know how to hear it. Francis was listening.

And what was this powerful voice saying as it re-echoed in the black night, interrupted only by the lightning? It decried the vanity of everything of this world. It affirmed that all things of the flesh are as the grass of the field which flourishes in the morning and shrivels under a burning wind later the same day. Again and again it repeated the same theme—but on a deeper note, quite muffled and reverberating, losing itself behind the great mountains. What else was this voice saying? That the glory with which God is surrounded is awful and that no one can see God until one dies and passes through water and fire.

Fire fell now from heaven—and soon water was mixed with it. At first a few large drops came—then it poured, a hard driving downpour which fell on the rocks, bounced off, then streamed from all sides toward the ravine, gurgling as it went. The water descended on the mountain like a giant baptism, like an invitation to a great purification.

Francis watched and listened. He stood motionless in the shelter of a rock; he had nothing else to do but watch and listen.

It was no longer the moment to go through the world preaching the Gospel to the crowds, no longer the time to assemble his brothers in order to admonish them. In fact, it was no longer a question of doing something but solely one of standing there—as the mountain stood, without budging, without flinching, in the oppressive night stabbed by lightning—concerned only with receiving the water and the fire of heaven and letting them purify him.

The voice was mysterious and difficult to hear.

The rain stopped. A fresh wind came up and whispered over the mountain. In the sky a few faint stars, distant and pallid, quivered and it seemed that at any moment the breeze might extinguish them. The night remained dark, very dark. Everything was merged in shadows and one could not distinguish this from that—neither a familiar rock nor a tree; there were only shapeless forms blending with the night. Characteristic silhouettes were effaced, leaving the eye to peer into a dark, bottomless void.

It is hard to accept this effacement of things and to maintain a conversation with what seems to be nothingness. It is hard to remain awake in the midst of empty darkness, where not only all familiar beings have lost their color, their voice and even their identity, but where the Divine Presence itself seems to have disappeared.

Francis had desired poverty. He had espoused it, as he used to say. And here, at this moment of his existence, he was poor—painfully poor—beyond all that he had ever dreamed.

Not long ago when he had withdrawn to this mountain, everything had spoken to him of God and God's grandeur. Untamed nature filled him with an awareness of the Divine Majesty. He had only to let himself be carried away by it, as the sea gull is borne by the wave.

At present, it was the hour of the ebbing tide and he was there, oppressed, gasping like the fish which struggles not to die.

3

The Last Star

A little while later, Brother Angelo arrived at the hermitage. His coming was entirely unexpected. The friar explained he had come on behalf of Sister Clare to invite Francis to visit her. She said she had a great need to see him, but was careful not to be more explicit.

Actually, if she desired to see Francis so much at that moment, it was because she could see—even from her faraway monastery of San Damiano—what was going on in the soul of her Father. She had been told that he had withdrawn to the mountains to rest, but she had soon understood that there must be something the matter. She knew how Francis felt about things, his grave concern over cares that were caused by an important faction of his community of friars. Something had warned her that the heart of her Father was in profound distress.

When Francis heard the name of Clare, his face suddenly brightened, although the brightness was extinguished almost immediately, like the lightning in the night. At that moment, the loveliest days of his life had been brought to his mind. The name of Clare was associated in his thoughts with a happy and luminous time when nothing equivocal ever tarnished the luster of the evangelical ideal that the Lord himself had revealed to him.

Better than anyone, Clare had perceived the hidden splendor of this way of life and she became so imbued with it that it radiated from her. What she had come to seek from Francis while she was still a young girl—this descendent from the noble family of the Offreduzzi—was indeed the pure simplicity of the Gospel. Francis had consecrated her to the Lord and Clare had remained faithful to her holy poverty.

"Blessed be the Lord for our Sister Clare!" exclaimed Francis, hearing Brother Angelo. But immediately he felt like adding, "Cursed be those who overthrow and demolish that which you, Lord, have built and continue to build through the holy brothers of this order!" He restrained himself, however, for those at whom he was aiming were not there to hear him. Moreover, cursing grieved him too much.

He only said to Brother Angelo, "Return to our Sister Clare and tell her that I am in no condition to go to her right now. Ask her, please, to excuse me. I bless her as much as . . . even more than I am able!"

Several days later, Francis experienced some feelings of regret. In order to show Sister Clare that he had not forgotten her and that he appreciated her gesture, he dispatched Brother Leo to her.

As soon as Clare saw Brother Leo coming, she hastened to ask him, "How is our Father?"

"Our Father," answered Leo, "still suffers very much with his eyes as well as with his stomach and liver, but it is his soul, above all, which is afflicted."

He was silent for an instant. Then he continued, "Our Father has lost joy—all joy. He tells us himself that his soul is bitter. Oh, if only those who are betraying his ideal knew how they are hurting him! They are putting his very life in jeopardy."

"Yes, our Father is in danger," said Clare, "but the hand of God has not been withdrawn from him; rather, it leads him. Assuredly, God wishes to purify him as gold in a furnace and he will return to us more resplendent than the sun. I have no doubt of it. The rising of the Lord in his soul is more certain than the coming of dawn on earth.

"But," she added, "we must surround and support him in this terrible trial, lest the bitterness take root in his heart. It is not enough for the seed to grow and bear fruit; we must take care lest the fruit be bitter. Bitterness lies in wait for all that is mature; it is the gnawing worm. There lies the danger, Brother Leo. I feel that if our Father could come here for a few days, it would do him a world of good. Do everything you can to make him leave his solitude."

Returning to the hermitage, Brother Leo went to Francis immediately and found him sitting near the small oratory. He conveyed to him, with much insistence, the invitation of Sister Clare.

"Our Sister Clare is praying for me and that is the essential thing," Francis replied gently. "She had no need to see me at this moment. She would see only a face clouded by shadow and sadness."

"Yes, Father," answered Leo, "but perhaps she could bring back a little of the brightness."

"It is the opposite which I fear," countered Francis. "I dread casting trouble and darkness into her soul. Leo, you do not know the thoughts that rack me. At certain times, I am haunted by the idea that I would have done better to stay at my father's business, to take a wife and to have children as everyone else does. And a voice repeats to me incessantly that it is still not too late to make good. Do you think I can go to our Sister Clare with ideas like that in my head?"

"These are ideas without foundation," said Leo. "They are wild imaginings, but they have no real hold on you. You could not be shaken and carried away by such ideas."

"No—well, get that idea out of your head," insisted

Francis. "I am indeed capable of it and I am still quite able to have sons and daughters."

"Father, what are you saying?" exclaimed Leo.

"Nothing but the truth," said Francis. "Why are you so astonished by it?"

"Because I consider you a saint," answered Leo.

"God alone is holy," retorted Francis. "For me, I am only a vile sinner. Do you hear, Brother Leo? A vile sinner! Only one thing is left to me in my night; it is the boundless compassion of my God. Only pray, Brother Leo, pray that in my darkness this last star may not be extinguished before my eyes."

Then Francis was silent. At the end of a moment, he got up and fled weeping into the wood. Leo watched him go.

4

The Groaning
of the Poor One

Several days later, returning to the hermitage from his prayer in the woods, Francis found a young brother waiting for him.

It was a lay brother who had come expressly to ask for a permission. The brother loved books so very much and he wished the Father would permit him to keep a few. He wanted especially to have a psalter. His piety, he explained, would increase if he were able to have such books at his disposal. He actually had the permission of his superior but he was anxious to have Francis approve.

Francis listened as the brother expounded his request. He could perceive much more than what the brother was saying. In fact, the brother's words resounded in his ears like an echo. He seemed to hear the language of certain ministers of his order, dazzled by the prestige of books and science. Had not one of them, not so long ago, begged for permission to reserve for his own use one whole collection of magnificent and precious books? Under the pretext of piety, brothers were being diverted from the humility and simplicity of their vocation.

But that was not enough—now innovators wanted Francis to give his approval. The authorization which he might grant this young brother would be eagerly exploited by the ministers.

Truly, it was too much! Francis felt a violent anger surging within, but he stiffened and restrained himself. He wished he were a thousand miles from there—far from the gaze of the brother who was waiting and watching for his reaction.

Suddenly an idea burst upon him. "You want a psalter!" he exclaimed. "Well, wait. I will get one for you." He bounded toward the kitchen of the hermitage which he entered and plunging his hand into the cinders on the hearth, picked up a handful of ashes and returned to the brother.

"Here you are—here is your psalter," he said.

And saying this, he rubbed the crown of the young one's head with the ashes.

The brother was not expecting this. Surprised and confused, he did not know what to think or say. It was obvious that he had not understood. He remained there silently with his head bowed. Francis himself, his first reaction past, felt abashed before this mute figure. He had spoken to him in harsh language, too harsh perhaps.

Now he would explain to him why he had acted that way and would speak his mind to him clearly and at length. He would show him that, assuredly, he had nothing against science, nor against property in general but that he knew, he the son of a rich clothing merchant of Assisi, how difficult it is to possess something and to remain the friend of all people—above all, the friend of Jesus Christ. Where each one endeavors to own property, it is the end of a true community of comrades and friends. Nothing under the sun can prevent someone who possesses something from spontaneously protecting it from others.

In days gone by, Francis had explained this to the bishop of Assisi who was appalled at the extreme poverty of the friars. "Lord Bishop," he had declared to him then, "if we had any possessions, we would need arms to defend them."

The Bishop had understood. These were things he knew by experience. Too often, clerics of the church had to change into soldiers-in-arms in order to defend their wealth and their rights.

But what connection did all this have with a psalter in the hands of a novice? Francis could readily see that in the eyes of this young brother, all these serious explanations could only appear out of proportion to the object of his request—out of proportion and, therefore, unintelligible. Never had Francis felt more helpless than at this moment!

"When you have your psalter," he said at last, hoping to make the brother understand, in spite of all, "what will you do with it? You will go and sit in your armchair like an exalted prelate on a throne and you will say to your brother, 'Bring me my psalter.' "

The brother smiled, an embarrassed smile, for he did not fathom the depth of the remark. Francis was trying to express for him, with humor, the tragedy of possession such as he saw it—when all human contacts, perverted and corrupted, are reduced to the relationship of ruler and slave because of property, because of wealth which we think we possess. And one need not possess very much to behave like an overlord. That indeed was deep, too deep for smiling.

But Francis had only a child standing before him—a poor child unable to understand these serious matters, but a child nevertheless whom he must try to save. He felt himself filled with an immense pity and he took the novice tenderly by the arm and led him to a rock where they sat down together.

"Listen, little brother," he said to him, "I am going to confide something to you. When I was younger, I too, was tempted by books and I would have loved to have some. I thought then that they would bring me wisdom. But all the books of the world, you see, are incapable of giving wisdom. You must not confuse science with wisdom. In bygone days, each and every devil knew more concerning celestial things—and today knows more about terrestrial things—than all people put together. At the hour of trial, in temptation or distress, it is not the books that will help us but simply the Passion of Our Lord, Jesus Christ."

Francis paused an instant. Then sorrowfully, he added. "At present I know Jesus, poor and crucified. That is enough for me."

This thought suddenly absorbed him completely. He remained there entranced with his eyes closed, out of all contact with everything around him. After a while, when he opened his eyes, he was startled to see that he was alone. The brother had left him and had gone away.

Days passed. To Francis they were becoming more and more gloomy, for the autumn had come. Great gusts of wind tore the leaves from the trees, leaves of yellow and purple which flew so high, whirling and dancing in the light of the sun like a swarm of butterflies. Little by little the forest lost its glamour and among the denuded trees, only the great dark pines still preserved an occasional touch of verdure. Soon the first frost was felt, announcing the immediate approach of winter. On a December morning, the hermitage awakened beneath the snow.

The setting was changing. But for Francis time

seemed to have stopped. Something within him had congealed. The days and seasons followed their cycle, but he was no longer in the rhythm of things and of beings. He was living outside of time. As he had often been seen before moving along the golden paths of autumn, he was now seen gliding like a shadow on the freshly fallen snow, always in search of the peace which eluded him.

Thus Francis passed long hours far from the sight of his brothers. He prayed—but it was not the way it used to be at the little churches in the countryside of Assisi, in San Damiano or at Portiuncula. Christ no longer came to life before his eyes. Instead, there was emptiness, a great void.

He asked himself what he should do. Leave the hermitage and return into the midst of all his brothers? But how then could he hide from them his sadness, his agony? And what could he say to them? Should he remain in solitude? But would that not be abandoning those whom the Lord had entrusted to him?

He felt responsible for each of his brothers, like a mother toward each of her children. How many would be disturbed, distracted and perhaps alienated from their vocation forever by his silence and his withdrawal? Now and then he felt anger welling up inside—anger against all who wished to tear his sons from him. Then he would even begin to doubt himself. He reproached himself for his faults, his pride above all.

While Francis was thus lost in solitude before God,

the hours slipped away. He frequently forgot to eat or arrived late for the office of the small community. The brothers became accustomed to not waiting for him. In fact, they had agreed not to wait.

The distress into which their Father was plunged overwhelmed them all and yet, when he was with them, he endeavored to conceal the deep feelings that tortured him. He appeared affable, attentive to each of them and exquisitely kind. He always had a good word for the brother who returned from his tour of beggary in the mountain hamlets. But he was not able to hide from them his eyes, reddened and scorched by tears, nor could he hide any longer how appallingly thin he had become. Everyone could see that he was truly fading away.

One bitterly cold day, Leo left to look for him in the snow. He found him kneeling against a rock with which he seemed to have become fused as one. He actually seemed to be petrified. Nearby, a tall pine tree all covered with snow and hoar-frost offered to the sky an enormous bouquet of glittering needles. It seemed like a colossal candelabrum of solid silver.

Leo helped Francis get up and gently led him back to the hermitage, supporting him by the arm as if he were a poor lost child. Here and there, clumps of snow glided down the high branches of the pines and landed in a noiseless explosion of fine white powder. A glacial cold held everything in its fierce embrace. In the silence, they could hear the trees crack under the bite of the frost. The oblique rays of a pale winter sun made the snow dazzling. The reflection blinded Francis, for his afflicted eyes were not able to endure such brilliance. He was like an owl flushed from its retreat, blinded by the light of day.

Leo led Francis to the hut where the brothers had lighted a fire. Francis sat down in front of the hearth, locking his hands under his knees, and there he remained for a long time contemplating the fire. He said nothing. Occasionally a shiver would run through him and he would shake visibly.

When the flame was not too bright, his eyes would follow its rapid movement and he would watch it run from one end of the half-burned log to the other. It would leap up, dance, then lie down and roll under the embers almost extinguishing itself, only to spring up anew with sudden cracklings bursting into showers of sparks. Now and then, Leo threw a handful of dry twigs into the fire in order to revive it. The flame would really leap up then, all bright and white. To avoid the brilliance, Francis either closed his eyes or screened them with his hands.

Leo spoke to him gently—sweet, simple words that one might speak to a sick child. Francis was listening and smiling. He felt exhausted, incapable of the least effort and he remained motionless with his gaze lost in the fire. The flame was dying down slowly, dividing into a hundred fragments, little flames of blue, green, red and orange, which scintillated from every part of the log, enveloping it and licking it with a feeble, plaintive sizzling. Outside, the gusts of wind howled and whistled while the forest groaned under its blast.

Francis was pensive in front of the meager fire. In days past, whenever the brothers would go into the forest for wood, he always earnestly advised them to spare the stump in the hope that the bush or tree would grow green again. Now, he was asking himself if the stump of his own life, its branches pruned back by suffering, would ever bear the foliage of joy again.

5

Still More Darkness

In winter, life is hard in the mountain hermitages. Solitude then becomes more intense, more formidable. One remains alone with all traces of life effaced, alone with one's thoughts and desires. Woe to them who seek such solitude without being led by the Holy Spirit. Day after day, dismal and cold, the solitary ones must remain enclosed in their cells. Outside the paths are either covered with snow or an endless icy rain falls.

There one is alone before God without any possible escape. Never a book to distract him, nor a companion to watch or encourage, there the hermits find themselves thrown back to their own resources, to their God or their demons. They pray, yes, and occasionally lend an ear to the world of nature outside the door, but even there it is no longer the call of the birds that one hears but the whistle of the north wind as it howls across the snow. One trembles from the cold, remembering that no food has been eaten, perhaps since morning. Then one begins to wonder if the others who have gone to beg will bring back something to eat.

When people are cold, they curl up like an animal. It may be that they even forget to meditate and instead mutter and blaspheme. Winter is always hard in the homes of the poor. Their roofs are too thin or too dilapidated to bar the cold drafts. The sharp north wind steals inside, right into the heart itself, which becomes so chilled that it shivers bitterly.

Even though someone has longed for poverty and feels as hard and durable as rock, the bite of the cold can sometimes get the better of one and crack the very stone itself. Then, insidiously, temptation speaks and its language is that of common sense: "What is the point of suffering so? Is it not sheer folly to insist upon enduring hunger and cold without reason? Is it truly necessary to withdraw into a dangerous situation in order to serve the Lord?"

In more favored souls, the temptation might assume another aspect, nobler and purer than common sense, that of holiness itself.

Of all the inhabitants of the hermitage, Brother Rufino was the one who studied Francis most. For months, he had watched Francis drag himself sadly around, without sparkle, without impetus, without joy. At the beginning, he had felt great compassion for Francis. Then he was rather puzzled; now he was concerned. This prolonged state of melancholy and prostration in Francis disturbed him. It was out of character.

Insidiously, doubt arose in Rufino's soul. Was Francis really the person of God that he had thought he was? Was Rufino not deceived in following him? Perhaps he had believed prematurely in his holiness. Perhaps it was for him, Brother Rufino, to take up the challenge and to show everyone what a true saint could do!

Then an angel of Satan, clothed in a robe of light, came to whisper in his ear, "Brother Rufino, what are you doing with this son of Pietro Bernardone? He is a stupid fellow who has tried to play the role of an innovator. He has seduced many and deluded himself. See what has happened—he is now nothing more than a limp rag, without energy, without willpower. And why does he languish and moan? Because of a great pride, wounded and disillusioned.

"Believe me. I am the Son of God. I know whom I have chosen and predestined. The son of Bernardone is damned and whosoever follows him is duped! Pull yourself together before it is too late. Let this innovator hasten to his ruin. Do not heed him any longer; do not even speak to him of the things I have just told you. Above all, beware of asking him any questions, for he might seduce you.

"But rather, go forward, boldly and simply! Follow your inclination for perfection—this yearning which I have placed in you as a pledge of eternity! The hermits of old, whose example you study, will show you the way. This is the sure way, tried and blessed. Imitate the ancients, then, and pay no attention to those who wish to change everything under the pretext of the Gospel."

And the angel of Satan flashed his magnificent cloak under Rufino's eyes. He was dazzled and delighted. Without the least doubt, God himself had just spoken to him by the mysterious voice.

From that day on, Rufino ceased to appear among the community. Like the ancient hermits, he wished to live in total isolation without seeing anyone. Above all, he wished to avoid meeting Francis for he had lost all confidence in him. Whenever, by chance, he would see Francis coming toward him, he would take off in another direction.

At first, neither Francis nor the other friars noticed Rufino's attitude. They all had a very high regard for their brother and they knew he was a person of profound contemplation. Francis had taught them to respect the individual designs of the Lord for each of them. He, himself, took great care not to interfere with the workings of God in the soul.

But one day a sudden turning in a mountain path brought Francis face-to-face with Rufino, who was startled by the encounter. He immediately made an about-face and, like a frightened animal, fled into the woods. Astonished, Francis called his name several times, but in vain.

Rufino's flight from him opened his eyes. Thought Francis, "It could not be the spirit of the Lord who made him run away, but rather the wicked one, who always seeks to separate someone from his brothers in order to drag him down more easily."

Several days later, after praying for a long time, Francis sent Leo to find Rufino.

"What do I have to do with Brother Francis?" protested Rufino to Leo, "I do not want to follow him any longer. I have had enough of his fantasies. Now I want to lead a solitary life in which I shall be able to save myself with more certainty than if I followed the nonsense of Brother Francis."

"What are you saying, Brother Rufino!" exclaimed Leo, who could not believe his ears.

"What I say scandalizes you, doesn't it?" said Rufino. "Francis is not the person of God that you believe he is. I now have the proof, absolute proof. For many months he has dragged himself about pitifully, without energy, without volition, without joy. Now tell me, is that the attitude of a saint? Certainly not!

"He has deceived himself and he has deceived us. You must remember that day when he compelled me in the name of obedience to preach half-naked and without a tunic in the church of Assisi. Do you believe that he was inspired by God? No! That was only a fantasy, a clown's whim among a thousand others! Well, those times are over for me. No longer will he send me to preach or to care for lepers. The Lord has shown me the way I am to follow."

"Who on earth has put these ideas into your head?" gasped Leo, quite overcome. "If God willed that you should endure, even for an instant, such things as our Father suffers in body and soul, you would immediately cry out for mercy. To hold on in the midst of such great sufferings as he has, indicates truly that the grace of God is sustaining him, that the strength of God is within him! Think about that for a moment."

"I have already thought about it," replied Rufino. "God himself has spoken to me. From henceforth my mind is made up about the son of Pietro Bernardone."

"No, no, it is not possible!" protested Leo, completely astonished. "Surely you are not going to abandon our Father! For you, it would mean damnation; and for him, what a mortal blow! I beg of you, Rufino, by the love of our Lord Jesus Christ, put aside these thoughts and return to us. We all need you. The devil knows it well; that is why he continues in his determination to seduce you."

"Go away, Brother Leo!" Rufino interrupted abruptly. "Do not bother me any longer. My way is completely outlined by the Lord himself. Leave me in peace. That is all I ask."

Leo returned to Francis and recounted his interview with Rufino. Francis then saw the grave danger that his brother was risking and he asked himself how he was going to be able to save him. He let several days go by, then once more he sent Leo for Rufino. But Leo ran into the same obstinacy and the same refusals and had to return without any more success.

"Alas! It is my fault," Francis lamented to Leo. "I have not been sufficiently attentive. I have not known how to draw him toward me. I have not suffered as I must while drawing others to me, as the Lord Jesus himself has suffered."

"Jesus, too, was abandoned by his own at the moment of his agony and passion," Leo remarked.

"Yes, it is true," said Francis after a moment of silence. " 'I will smite the shepherd,' it is written, 'and the sheep will be scattered.' God permitted this for his Son and the disciple should not try to be above the Master."

He was silent and remained absorbed in his thoughts for several moments. Leo looked at him, not knowing what to say.

"Ah, Brother Leo, this is truly the hour of darkness! This is horrible. I did not imagine that it could be so horrible. Leave me alone for now, Brother Leo. I must cry out to God."

Leo withdrew. Then Francis prayed:

"Lord God, you have snuffed out my lamp. I have

been plunged into darkness, and with me, all those you have given to me. I have become for them an object of terror. Those who were closest to me now flee from me. You have estranged my friends, my companions of the early days. O Lord, hear my prayer! Has the night not lasted long enough? Enkindle a new fire in my heart! Turn your face toward me and may the light of your dawn shine forth anew on my face so that those who follow me may not walk in darkness. Take pity on me beause of them."

Not far away, some snow slipped from the top of a tree. A cracking of branches could be heard, then a dull thud on the ground and there was great silence once more.

6

Can It Be the First Light of Dawn?

In the spring, as soon as the roads were passable again, Francis set out to see Sister Clare. He had finally yielded to the urging of Brother Leo. The winter that he had just spent at the hermitage had been the dreariest of any winter he had ever known. Yet in leaving the little mountain he was not bidding it farewell; he promised himself most fervently that he would return there as soon as possible. With Leo, his constant companion on journeys, he descended the wooded slopes which were already putting on a cloak of young green shoots. Beyond the hills, glistening with dew and sunshine, he reached the road which led to San Damiano.

Clare's joy was great indeed when they told her that

Francis was there. But when she saw his face, emaciated and gray, where one could read intense suffering, she was overcome with pity and sadness.

"Oh, Father," she said gently, "how you must have suffered! Why have you waited so long before coming to see us?"

"Sadness overwhelmed me, paralyzed me," Francis told her. "I have suffered terribly and there is more to come."

"Why, Father, do you sink to these depths of sadness?" asked Clare. "You can see how it hurts you, and the rest of us have such need of you—such need of your peace and joy."

"I would not be so grieved if the Lord had not placed such a large family under my care," replied Francis, "or if I did not feel myself responsible for my brothers in their faithfulness to their vocation."

"Yes. I understand," said Clare, who wished to spare him painful explanations.

But Francis was anxious to speak. He had a heavy heart and found it a relief to express himself freely.

"Today, our vocation is open to question," he resumed. "Many of the brothers are casting envious glances at those forms of religious life which are more organized, more powerful, better installed and they wish that we would adopt these forms. I am afraid that they are being pressured into this attitude by the fear of seeming inferior to the others. They are anxious to find for themselves a place in the sun. As for me, I have nothing against the forms of religious life of which the holy church approves, but the Lord did not call upon me to found a powerful order, nor a university, nor a war-machine against the heretics. A powerful order aims at a precise goal. It has something to do or to defend and it is organized accordingly. It must be strong to be effective. The Lord has not asked us, the Friars Minor, to do, or reform, or defend anything in the holy church. He himself has revealed to me that we must live according to the formula of the Holy Gospel. To live—yes, simply just to live. But to live fully, by following the humility and poverty of the Most High Lord Jesus Christ, by leaving aside all designs for domination, all preoccupation with buildings and prestige, all special desires of any kind. I have reflected on this at length during my retreat on the mountain this winter. It has become evident to me that our life according to the way of the Holy Gospel is of such a nature that one cannot apply to us the organization principles of other orders without destroying our life in the process. Our way of life does not lend itself to molding or regulation from the outside. This evangelical life, if it is lived in an authentic manner, ought to spring up freely and find its law in itself. Certain brothers ask me for a more precise rule, better defined. However, I am not able to tell them one thing more than what I have already told them and what the Holy Father has fully approved—that is the rule and the life of the Friars Minor must consist in observing the Holy Gospel of our Lord Jesus Christ. Even today, I have nothing to add or to retract. Let the brothers live, then, in a humble and poor condition just like the Lord. Let them proclaim the Kingdom of God to all creatures, just as he did, and if they are driven away or persecuted in one place, let them go somewhere else. But wherever they are received, let them eat whatever anyone offers them. The brothers who live this way will not constitute a powerful order, no doubt, but they will be the true children of the Gospel. They will be free people because nothing will limit their horizon and the spirit of the Lord will breathe within them as God wishes."

Clare listened, deeply moved. She hid her emotions with difficulty. All that she heard echoed deep in her soul and all that she saw completely upset her. While speaking, Francis had grown more and more animated and this frail, wasted person who seemed to have lost all comeliness was radiant at that moment with an ethereal beauty. His words gave him an aura of strength and greatness. A mighty passion aroused and illuminated him. It was a prophet who was speaking.

Clare would have been content with admiring and approving, but she was not able to forget that at this moment she had an important part to play. To her eyes, the extraordinary greatness which then invested Francis was highlighted by the suffering that haunted him. Clare let him speak because she could see that this was a relief for him. Yet, while she was listening, she constantly asked herself how she might take him by the hand and put him back on the road to peace.

As for Francis, he was entirely absorbed in his subject and no longer felt the burning of his eyes or his stomach. He had a sense of rejuvenation; all his sufferings were ameliorated by the passion which quickened him. At that moment, he would have willingly undertaken a journey over the entire earth to see the realization of the Lord's will for him. However, he was planning without considering his physical strength, a strength no longer equal to the flame which consumed him. While he was speaking, a great fatigue suddenly spread over him and with this lassitude, dejection soon reentered his soul. Once more, the black butterflies began to dance before his ailing eyes.

"Alas," he continued after a short moment of silence, "I am like a father rejected by his own children. They no longer know me. They blush because of me; my simplicity makes them ashamed. May the Lord have pity on me, Sister Clare."

"All your children have not rejected you," corrected Clare gently, "and God always leads you by the hand."

"Even God!" sighed Francis sadly. "When I am in solitude now and present myself to him, I am afraid and I tremble. If only I knew what I ought to do!"

"Perhaps there is nothing to do," countered Clare.

After a moment of silence, Clare resumed, "You know that in the Gospel the Lord said, 'The kingdom of heaven

is like the person who has sown good grain in a field.'
The wheat grew, but so did the weeds. When the servants came to ask the owner if they should not set about
pulling out the weeds, the owner replied, 'Do nothing
about it, since you risk pulling out both the wheat and
the weeds. Leave them there to grow together until the
harvest.'

"God does not share our fears, or our pride, or our
impatience. God knows how to wait as only God can wait,
as only an infinitely good parent knows how to wait. God
is long-suffering, merciful, always filled with hope until
the very end. It is of little importance to God if mounds
of waste accumulate in the field and make it ugly to see.
This is of little importance if at the harvest God can reap
much more wheat than weeds.

"As for us, we find it hard to think that weeds may
one day change into wheat and yield the glorious russet
or golden grain. The farmers will tell you that they have
never seen a similar transformation in their fields. But
God who does not look at appearance knows that with
time and in God's mercy, God can change the hearts of
people.

"There is a time for all beings but time is not the
same for all. The time for inanimate things is not the
time of the animals, and that of animals is not that of
humans. Above all and different from all, there is God's
time which encompasses all others and surpasses them.
The heart of God does not beat at the same rate as ours.

It has its own rhythm, that of God's eternal mercy which extends from age to age and never grows old. It is very difficult for us to enter into the divine tempo—and yet only there are we able to find peace."

"You are right, Sister Clare. My trouble and my impatience stem from roots that are too human. I can see that clearly but I have not yet discovered God. I do not yet live in God's time."

"Who dares to pretend that they live in God's time?" Clare asked. "For that, one would need the very heart of God."

"To learn to live in God's time," resumed Francis. "there, without doubt, is the secret of wisdom."

"And the source of very great peace," added Clare.

Once more there was a moment of silence, then Clare added, "Suppose that one of the sisters of this community came to confess that she had broken some object through awkwardness or carelessness. I would, no doubt, make some remark and give her a penance, as is the custom. But suppose she had come to tell me that she had set the convent on fire and that everything was burned or nearly so. I believe that at that moment I would not be able to say a thing. I would be faced with an event that would overwhelm me. The destruction of the convent is truly too great a catastrophe for me to cope with. That which God has built cannot depend on the will or caprice of a creature. It is a different order of magnitude."

"Oh, if only I had faith as great as a grain of mustard

seed," sighed Francis.

"You would say to this mountain, 'Remove yourself from there,' and the mountain would vanish," added Clare.

"Yes, it is really so," agreed Francis. "But at present I have become like a blind person and someone must take me by the hand to lead me."

"One is not blind who sees God," replied Clare.

"Alas!" cried Francis. "In my darkness I feel my way and see nothing."

"But God leads you in spite of all," Clare reassured him.

"I believe it, truly, in spite of all," said Francis.

They heard the birds singing in the garden. From the plains in the distance, a donkey brayed. A bell tolled.

"The future of this large religious family that the Lord has given to my care," resumed Francis, "is assuredly too great a thing to depend on me alone and to preoccupy me to distraction. Besides, it is, above all, God's affair. You have expressed it well, but pray that this counsel may at last germinate in me like a seed of peace."

Francis remained at San Damiano for several days. Thanks to Clare's attentive ministrations, he regained a little strength. In the peace of the convent and the soft light of an Umbrian springtime, Francis seemed to have given a holiday to his cares and worries. It pleased him to hear the song of the larks and he watched them in an immense sky of deep blue until they were lost to sight.

At night, retiring to a hut at the far end of the garden, he passed moments of sleeplessness at his small window studying the heavens scintillating with stars. Never before had the stars seemed so lovely to him. It was as if he were discovering them for the first time. They twinkled with a clear and rare brilliance in the vast nocturnal silence. Nothing troubled them. No doubt they belonged to God's time for they had neither will nor movement of their own. They simply obeyed the rhythm of God and that was why nothing could trouble them. They were in the peace of God.

In the midst of all this, Francis was dreaming of getting back to the hermitage. He was thinking of the brothers he had left up there, above all of Brother Rufino who, he knew, was in grave danger. Easter was very near. He was eager to return in order to be with his brothers and to join them in celebrating the Resurrection of Christ.

At the moment of departure, Clare said to Francis, "Would you indulge us, Father? It is just a little something. The sisters gathered flower seeds last autumn. These are from some magnificent flowers and they will grow very easily. Here they are in this little bag. Take them and sow them high on your mountain."

Clare knew that Francis loved flowers very, very much and she thought they would help him banish the bitter plants from his heart.

"Thank you," said Francis, taking the small packet of seeds. "I am delighted to have them and I shall surely sow them."

Then, with Leo, he bade farewell to Clare and her sisters.

The return journey did seem shorter to Francis. He walked with a livelier step. In a way barely perceptible, something in his being had been set back in motion. He was still suffering, no doubt, but no longer in the same way. Now his suffering was not so intense. As he walked, Clare's words haunted him. "The destruction of a convent—truly, that would be too great a catastrophe for me to cope with." And these words poured a little serenity into his heart.

After walking for a considerable time, Francis and Leo left the road to take the path which climbed under the beech trees and the oaks and led on to the hermitage.

All about them spring was bursting forth. The massive trees were unfolding their bright new foliage and the rays of the sun played on the soft green and gold of the tender leaves, while the song of the birds seemed to be everywhere. From the undergrowth, humid and warm, came a delightful odor of moss, dead leaves and violets in flower. Here and there, gay clumps of small red cyclamen were just appearing. No doubt these, too, were living and resting in God's time—God's time from the beginning.

The earth with its secret life had not excluded itself from God's time any more than did the stars of the heaven. The huge trees of the forest opened out their new leaves to the breath of God, just as on the first day of creation and with the same quivering freshness. Humans alone had departed from their original state. They had tried to chart their own course and live in their own time. Then they no longer knew rest but only weariness, trouble and the headlong course toward death.

At one point, the path that Francis and Leo were following cut across a roadway used by the farmers of the mountain and surrounding hamlets when they went up or down with their carts. Just at that moment, one of them was coming down, walking beside two large white oxen harnessed to a cart.

It was Paolo, small, stocky, with a florid complexion and a good-natured look. He lived in a hamlet that the brothers of the hermitage visited rather frequently, but he happened to drink a bit more than his share. At home, his wife kept an eye on him all the time. So, when he had a chance to go down to the village, he went there in good spirits as if on a holiday.

"Good morning!" he called out, seeing the two brothers.

"Good morning to you, Paolo," answered Leo, who recognized him immediately.

"It is always a pleasure to meet the brothers," said the farmer, halting his oxen.

"Are you on your way to the village, Paolo?" asked Leo.

"Oh! Yes, I have to go," answered the farmer, shrugging his shoulders. "My oxen need to be shod; my cart needs to be repaired and then," he added with a sprightly and knowing air, "there is Paolo, too, who needs a small sip of good wine."

This declaration from someone so guileless and good-natured amused Francis, who laughed aloud. "Well, go then, Paolo," he said. "That is fine. You are at least honest. A small sip of good wine cannot hurt you. But beware! Be careful. You must not multiply those sips too much."

The farmer laughed with a light heart. Then suddenly staring at Francis, he assumed a grave aspect.

"Aren't you Brother Francis?" he asked. "The brothers from the hermitage who came to our house collecting told us that Brother Francis was now living with them up there on the mountain."

"I am," answered Francis simply.

"Well," said the farmer in an almost confidential tone, patting him in a friendly way on the shoulder, "try to be as good as they say you are. Many people have put their trust in you—don't let them down."

"God alone is good, Paolo," answered Francis. "For me, I am only a sinner. Listen carefully, dear friend. If the worst of rogues had received as much grace as I have, that person would have overtaken me in holiness by a hundred laps."

"What about me?" challenged the farmer jokingly.

"Could I become a saint?"

"Of course, Paolo," said Francis. "You, too, are loved by God just as I am. To believe in this love is enough for you to see your heart change."

"The likes of us are very far from all these things," mused the farmer. "You must come to see us, though. We certainly have great need of you. Well, see you soon, I hope."

And with one hand, he tapped the oxen on the rump to make them start and with the other hand, he waved farewell to the brothers.

Francis and Leo soon arrived at the summit of the first hill and from there they could see the small mountain rising in front of them. It had recovered its verdure and it stood clearly before their eyes against a sky of intense blue. All around, small valleys covered with olive trees resembled green paths narrowing in their ascent among the dry slopes of the mountains. Here and there, beds of yellow jonquils, like specks of gold, were shimmering in the sunlight. Over there, blocking the horizon, the chain of mountains cut into the blue with their bare rounded masses, all streaming with sunshine.

"How beautiful it is!" Francis exclaimed suddenly. "And in a few days the glory of the risen Lord will shine forth over all. Brother Leo, can't you hear the tremendous murmur of all creation which in its very depths is rehearsing the Alleluia Song for Easter?"

7

A Lark Sings Above the Spring Plowing

It was the beginning of Holy Week. The whole of Christendom was in solemn preparation for the mystery of the death and resurrection of the Lord. People stopped their labors and silenced their quarrels. They were free to attend the liturgical ceremonies which were as much a part of their life as working and quarreling, but a much deeper part.

They knew the need to wash themselves in the Blood of Christ. It was almost a physical need of renewal, rejuvenation and resurrection. Even in the most remote villages, in every hamlet where there was a minister, Christians were avidly celebrating the Lord's Eucharist and letting the grace from these sacraments permeate them with new purity and new vigor. It was then that Christianity grew green again, in a new spring.

At the hermitage, too, there were preparations for celebrating Easter. The members felt an equal need to refresh themselves. On Holy Thursday, Francis invited his brothers to celebrate the Lord's Supper together. They would all receive at the same Holy Sacrifice, after which they would join in a community breakfast.

On extending this invitation, Francis was thinking of Brother Rufino more than of anyone else because all during Lent he had kept apart from the community. Brother Leo went to convey the invitation from Francis.

"Tell Brother Francis that I will not come," Rufino answered. "And furthermore, I no longer wish to follow him. I want to remain here alone, for I will save myself more surely this way than in following the caprices of Brother Francis. The Lord himself has told me so."

When Francis heard this, it brought him deep sorrow. He immediately sent Brother Sylvester to try to persuade Brother Rufino to come, but Rufino was stubborn in his refusal.

Thus they had to begin the celebration of the Lord's Supper without him. His absence, however, tortured Francis and before the elevation of the Host, he dispatched a third brother to Rufino.

"Go, tell him to come at least to see the Body of Christ."

But Rufino did not budge any more than did the rock

where he had buried himself.

After Communion, unable to contain his sadness any longer, Francis withdrew and wept.

"How long, Lord," he groaned, "will you permit my guileless sheep to stray?"

Then suddenly he got up and went to Rufino's retreat himself. When Rufino saw Francis in the distance coming toward him, he was startled, but he did not stir.

"Oh, Brother Rufino, why have you caused me this great grief? I have sent for you three times and each time you have refused to come. And on such a day! Why? Tell me why!" pleaded Francis.

In his words there was no hint of reproach. It was the anguish of a mother that was speaking. At that moment, all his being reached out to Rufino and, holding his breath, he watched anxiously for the least expression on his brother's face. Oh, what would he not do to help him open his heart!

"I have told you," answered Rufino in a tone somewhat peevish, somewhat uneasy. "It seems safer to me to follow the rule of the ancient hermits rather than your fantasies. If I listened to you, I would be constantly distracted from my life of prayer. That is what happened in the past when you sent me to preach here and there or to care for the lepers. No, that is not what the Lord wishes for me. My salvation will be achieved through prayer in solitude, far from people, far from everything."

"But on this day when the Lord himself yearned to

share the Passover with his brothers, you could not possibly refuse us the pleasure of coming to eat with us," Francis said to him.

"I assure you, I see nothing worthwhile in it. I prefer to remain alone as the Lord has taught me," answered Rufino.

"The Lord is there where your brothers are," replied Francis gently. "Come, Brother Rufino, I beg of you by the love that is God incarnate, give me that joy. All your brothers are waiting for you; they cannot start without you."

"All right, so be it," said Rufino as he jumped up abruptly. "I will go since you insist so much." Then he added in a grumbling tone, "But I am not giving up my plan. I will return here as soon as possible."

During breakfast, Francis seemed quite relaxed. He had seated Rufino near him and spoke to him amicably as if nothing had ever happened and as if Rufino were really there not only physically but in spirit. Not even for a moment was there the thought of lecturing him.

Actually Francis had never known how to lecture anyone. He was too aware of his own misery and, more than that, he was too guileless. His words and attitudes were not dictated from without. He lived too deeply, too intensely and this fullness of life and goodness found its way to the exterior without the least premeditation as it followed its own natural rhythm.

Rufino was touched by this welcome—much more

touched than he dared show. But he had his own idea and he did not want to let it go. Moreover, was it not from God? He must therefore follow it—to the very end. He took leave of his brothers in a rather abrupt manner with his face somber and set.

Francis watched him leave without saying a word. He did not take his eyes from him, hoping to the very last that he would give a backward glance.

If Rufino had turned around at that moment he would have seen two arms extended toward him, two wide-open arms that could not leave him but stayed with him, sustaining him even while he strayed.

Rufino disappeared, but Francis remained standing there for a long time, watching. Then his arms dropped to his side, heavy with sadness. For a moment, he had rejoiced at being able to restore Rufino to the midst of his brothers. How fleeting was this conquest! His child was turning his back on him, escaping from him. How long must this go on?

Francis sat down at the base of a rock. The cuckoo was singing in the woods and the air was balmy and golden. But Francis did not see the sun, or hear the cuckoo. He was chilled. He was thinking of Brother Rufino and the others, all the others. If one of his first companions such as Rufino could turn away from him so easily, what loyalty could he expect from the rest of the congregation who hardly knew him?

The wound in his soul which Clare had dressed so

carefully was suddenly reopened and was bleeding. Fifteen years of effort, of vigilance and exhortations had led to this! He had labored in vain; he was a failure, a complete failure! He did not take it as a blow to his personal honor but as an offense to God, to the honor of God.

On the following day, Good Friday, Francis wished to spend the entire day in solitude, meditating on the Passion of Jesus. For this, he had chosen a desolate place where austerity was in harmony with the great thoughts which filled his soul. Anxious to participate in the feelings of the Lord, he began to recite slowly the Psalm that Jesus had uttered on the cross. He stopped at each verse for as long as it took the Word to reach to the depths of his being. Before the Word he was, as always, defenseless. He let it come to him and bear down on him with all its weight. But at last, it was the Word which supported him each time and uplifted him.

Now, while he was saying the words, "My God, my God, why hast thou forsaken me?" he was seized as never before by the feeling of extreme abandonment wrung from the Savior himself. All of a sudden, Francis felt as one with Christ, painfully one. Never before had he understood these words as he did now. They were no longer foreign.

For months he had searched for the face of God. For months he had lived with the impression that God was gone from him and from his order. The agony of the Son—

now he knew something of what it was. Why, it was the absence of the Father, a feeling of failure, an inevitable and absurd unfolding of events when those with a will for good are swept away and crushed by an interplay of inexorable forces.

The words of the Psalm slowly penetrated his soul. It did not hurl Francis back on himself, nor did it encompass him in his suffering. On the contrary, it made him receptive in the very depths of his being to the suffering of Christ. He felt that he had never contemplated this suffering except from the outside. Now he was seeing it from within. He was participating in it, testing it for himself as a personal experience until it nauseated him. This time at least, he was fully assimilated into Christ.

It had been a long time since he had first desired to imitate the Lord in a total way. Since his conversion, he had striven toward this goal relentlessly. Yet, he could see clearly at this moment that in spite of all his efforts, he still did not know what it was like to become completely like the Lord, or how far the experience could go. How could he know? People truly know only what they try. To follow Christ barefoot, clothed in one tunic, without staff, without purse, without provisions—surely this was something. But it was only a beginning, a starting point. Now he must follow it to the end and, like Christ, permit himself to be led by God across an abyss of abandonment to taste in hideous solitude the atrocious death of the Son of God.

The whole of Good Friday was exhausting. Francis found it very long, but then evening came bringing its peace, a peace deep as that which falls slowly on the plowed fields when the hard work is done. The ground is broken, it no longer offers the least resistance, but stretches out, open and docile. And then the cool of evening penetrates it and freshens it.

While returning to the hermitage, Francis felt this peace envelop him and little by little permeate his whole being. All was consummated. Christ was dead. He had rendered himself to his God in a radical abandonment. He had accepted failure. Human life, human honor, human suffering itself became effected before his eyes and to Francis all these things had ceased to matter. There remained only one immense reality—God. That alone was important. It sufficed that God is God. All his being was bowed before this sole reality. He adored the One. He had surrendered himself in this acceptance without reservation, in this extreme poverty and acquiescence. And the glory of God had seized him.

Beyond and above the mountains the sun was sinking slowly. Its rays sifted through the wood where Francis trudged. The forest was crossed by dazzling streaks and the trees were bathed in a vapor of light. A great calm prevailed. Not a whisper was heard. The hour was one of majestic serenity.

"God is. That suffices," murmured Francis.

In a clearing he looked up at the sky. It was cloudless. A great red bird, a milan, was gliding there and its tranquil, solitary flight seemed to say to the earth, "God alone is all powerful; God is eternal. It is enough that God is God."

Francis felt his soul lift, powerful and light at the same time, just like a wing. "God is. That suffices," he repeated.

These simple words in a strange way flooded his soul with a new light. They held for him an infinite resonance and Francis lent an ear. A Voice was calling him. It was not a human voice. There was a ring of compassion about it and it was speaking to his heart.

"Poor little person!" the Voice said. "Know well that I am God and worry no more. Is it because I have made you shepherd of my flock that you forget I am chief Shepherd? I have chosen you especially, a simple soul, so that it may be manifest to all that what I am working in you has nothing to do with your ability but with my grace. It is I who called you. It is I who watch the flock and provide the pasture. I am the Lord and the Shepherd. It is my concern; therefore do not be troubled."

"God, dear God!" exclaimed Francis gently. "You are our protection, our guardian, our defense. Great and admirable Lord, you are our all. Amen. Alleluia."

His soul brimmed over with peace and joy. He walked with a happy step; in fact, he was dancing rather than walking.

He arrived at a spot where the view extended far out

over the wide countryside. The panorama included the neighboring hills and beyond these, the plains which faded into the horizon. Francis stopped a moment to gaze at the scene.

On one of the hills, a herd of cows was heading home. They appeared rather diminutive, both the animals and the herders who walked behind them. No doubt there were dogs running around them too, but one could scarcely discern them. When one of the animals strayed from the group, how quickly it was turned back as if by an invisible force! The herder must have called out and the dogs must have barked, but at this distance and height one could not hear these things.

The scene was mute and appeared to be flowing through the silent life of nature. Here, the bustle of people was restored to its proper proportions. It was something very small, almost insignificant.

"You, God, alone are great," said Francis and he resumed his walk.

The day drew to a close. Fog was lifting from the crevices and filling the ravines as the stars began to appear in the sky. It has been this way since the beginning of time, he thought, as long as there has been night. It was a symbol of the permanence of God.

As he approached the hermitage, Leo came to meet him. "You have a joyous air this evening," Leo said to him.

"This evening there is a great open sky within me,"

answered Francis, "and in that sky an invisible lark is singing passionately of the victory of the Lord."

An hour later, as Francis was kneeling in the small oratory of the hermitage, he felt someone tug at his sleeve. He looked up and there was the face of Rufino bending toward him.

"Oh, Brother Rufino!" exclaimed Francis.

"Good evening, Father," said Rufino with a broad grin. "I would like to speak to you—not right now, but in a few days, if you are willing."

"Whenever you wish," Francis told him. "You know that I am always here. But, Brother Rufino, it seems that you have found joy again."

"Yes, Father, and that is what I wanted to tell you this evening without waiting a moment longer. The rest can be told later."

"God be praised!" cried Francis, jumping up. And he embraced him.

8

If We Know How To Adore

Easter was celebrated with joy at the hermitage. Brother Rufino had once more found the way back to the community and they saw him wreathed in smiles as never before. He was constantly searching for some way to render service. In the morning it was now he who was the first down at the spring to draw the water supply for the day. He would help in the kitchen and at sundry other tasks. He even offered himself for the round of collections and that was truly unusual for him. He seemed to be a person transformed and because of it, the atmosphere of the small community was overflowing with happiness.

On Easter Wednesday, Brother Rufino drew Francis aside and began to pour out his heart to him. "I have come to see you, Father, as I promised. I am just getting over a very bad period, but even now things are so much better. I realize now that I almost lost the meaning of my vocation."

"Tell me, then, what has happened," Francis urged.

Rufino was silent for an instant. He sighed like someone who has too many things to say and does not know where to begin. The two brothers were walking quietly under the pines not far from the hermitage. They moved without a sound on a thick carpet of dry needles. It was a mild day and the odor of balsam floated on the air.

"Let us sit here," said Francis. "It will be easier to talk."

They sat down on the ground and then Rufino began to tell his story. "When I came to ask you to admit me to your group of friars about twelve years ago, I was prompted by a desire to live according to the Holy Gospel in the way I saw you practice it. I was then very sincere and I wished truly to follow the Gospel. My first years in the brotherhood passed without too much difficulty. I applied myself with zeal to all that this new life seemed to require of me.

"But in the depths of my being, without knowing it, I was motivated by a spirit that was far from evangelical. You know the environment in which I grew up. I was of a noble family. By my sensitivity, by my education and by all the vibrant fibers of my being, I belonged to this noble society. I felt and judged according to its standards and the values ordinarily honored there. In coming to you and adopting your mode of life, so extremely humble and poor, I thought I had renounced those values for all time. I really thought I had lost myself to the Lord.

"It was true, but only on the surface. I had indeed changed my way of life and my occupation and for me it was a great change. But deep within myself, without realizing it, I was reserving a large part of my soul—the more important part. I retained my former state of mind, the product of my former environment. I continued to judge people and things according to the standards of my home and family. At my father's estate, receiving people at the door, working in the kitchen or at other chores, were the duties of domestics or valets. As a Friar Minor, I judged things the same way and to act as doorkeeper or cook, to go begging or to care for lepers was to lower oneself to an inferior state. Despite that, I would accept these assigned tasks willingly, precisely in order to humiliate myself. I even made it a point of honor to abase myself in this way. I thought this was evangelical humility and in this spirit I had entered the order.

"The years passed. Since I did not have the aptitude for preaching, I often saw myself reduced to discharging obligation which I deemed inferior or vile. Since it was my duty, I forced myself to do these things. I humbled myself through sheer duty and truly, I was humiliated.

"What was bound to happen, happened. I naturally began to think that the other brothers, who went out to preach, considered me their servant. This feeling was further enhanced when brothers younger than I and born in quite modest circumstances joined the order and were sent to preach, leaving to me the material welfare of the community. If one of those brothers made a remark or simply expressed a desire, I was bothered and irritated. I said nothing but I fumed inside. After a bit, I would take hold of myself and calm down. Then would I humble myself a little more, always through duty.

"Thus I did everything for duty's sake. To me that was the religious life. But it was only a poorly fitting suit which I tried hard to make fit but which I couldn't wear. Every chance I had, I took it off. My life, my true life, was elsewhere. It was there where I was completely myself. Each day I had only one desire—to have my vile tasks finished in order to take refuge in solitude. There I felt myself my own master, once more, and I was revived. When duty caught up with me again, I forced myself to be the servant of the others once again.

"However, a person can wear out in such a routine. It is incredible how tense one can become. All that I did for duty's sake, I did without heart—like a convict who drags around chains. I lost my appetite and forgot how to sleep. I began the day exhausted and developed a dislike for everyone in the community. I saw each of them as a ruler and myself as the slave.

"I felt unappreciated and that revolted me. I could no longer stand anyone. I was in inner turmoil against everyone. Then, in my inexperience, I honestly believed that the Lord wanted me all to himself in complete solitude. At that point, I asked you for permission to withdraw to this hermitage. Then, even here, there was the terrible crisis you saw. I had come to this!"

"Nothing that you tell me surprises me," said Francis gently. "Do you recall the day I sent you to preach in spite of yourself? I wanted to draw you out of your shell, out of the isolation where I felt you were imprisoned."

"Yes, Father, I remember. But I was unable to understand. It is curious that now all this is clear for me," answered Rufino.

"The Lord has taken pity on you," said Francis. "The Lord takes pity on each of us in God's own time. At the moment when we least expect it, we discover God's loving kindness. God is made known to us in this way, as the long-awaited rain settles the dust on the road."

"It is so true," remarked Rufino. "I have the feeling of beginning a new existence."

"But how did the Lord open your eyes?" Francis asked him.

"On Holy Thursday when we were together at breakfast," answered Rufino, "a member of the community recalled, incidentally, that you had said, 'If a mother nourishes and cherishes a child according to the flesh, how much more ought we to nourish and cherish one another according to the spirit?' I had often heard you say that, but I never paid any attention to it. And to tell the truth, I did not understand it. This time, the words became filled with meaning. I was struck by them, and when back in my cell, I meditated on them for a long time.

"In a family where there are no servants and things are simple, I said to myself, it is the mother who becomes the cook, who serves at table, manages the household and is bothered at every moment. She finds that quite normal. She does not consider herself degraded; she does not think of herself as a servant. She loves her children and her husband: hence her zest and courage to serve them. She may be tired, perhaps exhausted, but never revolted. I thought of a family of modest means that I had known fairly well where the mother, despite all her arduous tasks, radiated peace and happiness in the midst of her fatigue.

"It became clear to me then that I was traveling in the wrong direction, that I was led by a state of mind far from evangelical from which stemmed my resentment. I fancied that I had left the world because I had changed occupations. I had forgotten to change my soul. That moment was for me a complete turn-about in perspective.

"I did not wait a minute to take advantage of the light which had been shed on me. I immediately ran to place myself in the service of my brothers and ever since then the light has been growing brighter in me and so has peace. At the moment I feel as unburdened and free as a bird escaped from its cage."

"You can thank the Lord," Francis said to him. "What you have just gone through is an experience, indeed. You know now what a Friar Minor is—a poor one—according to the Gospel, a person who has freely renounced the exercise of all authority, any kind of domination over others, but nevertheless a person who is not led by a captive soul but by the most noble spirit that ever could be—the spirit of the Lord. The way is difficult. Few find it. It is a grace, a very great grace, which the Lord has given you.

"You see, it is not only the rulers of the world who are motivated by the will for power and domination. It is also true of servants who do not freely accept their lot as servants. This condition is then a heavy yoke which oppresses people and makes them resentful. The yoke is certainly not that of the Lord.

"To be poor according to the Gospel is not only to undertake the task of the lowest slave but to do it with the soul and spirit of the Lord. That makes all the difference. Wherever the spirit of the Lord abounds, the heart is not bitter. There is no room for resentment.

"When I was still in the world, I thought the lowest thing was to care for the lepers. But the Lord took pity on me and led me among them and I was compassionate toward them. As I left their midst, what had previously seemed bitter had changed into a sweet cleanliness of soul and body. The spirit of the Lord is not a spirit of bitterness but of sweetness and sparkling joy."

"This experience through which I have just lived has taught me how easy it is to be deluded about oneself," said Rufino. "How easy it is to mistake an impulse of nature for an inspiration of the Lord—and without shame!"

"Yes, self-delusion is all too easy," said Francis. "That is why it is so common. Nevertheless, there is a sign which permits us to identify it with assurance."

"What is that?" inquired Rufino.

"It is the turmoil of the soul," answered Francis. "When water becomes turbid, it is evident that it is not pure. The same holds for people. Individuals who are suffused by anxiety show that the source of inspiration for their actions is not pure; it is contaminated. Such persons are deeply moved by things other than the spirit of the Lord. As long as people have all they want, they cannot tell for sure whether or not the spirit of God leads them.

"It is so easy for them to raise their vices to the height of virtues and to delude themselves under the guise of noble and selfless goals. And all the while, totally unaware! However, when occasions arise and those who have deceived themselves are contradicted or opposed, their masks fall off. They are flustered and irritated. Behind the 'spiritual' façade appears their 'carnal' nature still very much alive, with claws bared for self-defense. This turmoil and this aggressiveness reveal that such persons are guided by deep motives other than those of the Lord."

The hermitage bell tolled; it was time to say the Office. Francis and Rufino arose and made their way toward the oratory. They went tranquilly, as do free people.

Suddenly Francis seized Rufino's arm and stopped him. "Listen, Brother; I must tell you something."

He paused an instant, gazing down at the ground. He seemed to hesitate. Then looking Rufino directly in the eye, he said to him gravely, "With the aid of the Lord, you have overcome your desire for power and prestige. But you will have to do it not just once, but ten, twenty, a hundred times."

"You frighten me, Father," said Rufino. "I am not cut out to withstand such a struggle."

"It is not in struggling you succeed," replied Francis gently, "but in adoring. The person who adores God knows that there is only one All-Powerful One. Such a person acknowledges it and accepts it deeply, heartily, and rejoices that God is God. God is. That is enough and that makes a peron free. Do you understand?"

"Yes, Father, I understand," answered Rufino. They had resumed their walk while still speaking and now were just a few steps from the oratory.

"If we knew how to adore, then nothing could truly disturb our peace," said Francis. "We would travel through the world with the tranquility of the great rivers."

9

One Must Despise Nothing

At the hermitage it was apparent to everyone that Francis had found peace once more. However, each of them felt certain that this peace in no way lightened the suffering in their Father's heart; peace had only transfigured it. Francis no longer gave the impression of a broken person. His face was again wonderfully open and radiant.

Often, in the course of the day, they could hear him singing and this made the community happy. And yet, to them he remained the person who had returned from the depths. He had advanced toward God as far as a person could go without dying. All alone, he had wrestled with the angel in the night—and he had triumphed. Now he was given back to his brothers, carrying the mysterious mark of this unequal struggle. The light which radiated from his glance banished every trace of shadow from his face, but it could not efface the expression of gravity where they could read the immensity of a soul which God had hollowed out in order that the Lord might dwell there more at ease.

Francis had resumed his solitary meditations. On the small paths under the pines, the vivid light of spring was gently filtered and became extremely soft. He loved to reflect and pray there. He said nothing, or almost nothing, for his prayers were not of a set formula at all. He listened more than anything else and was content to be there and to pay attention.

It might be said that he kept the watch like a hunter. He persevered through long hours of waiting, attentive to the least movement of every creature and every natural thing which surrounded him, ever ready to discover the least sign of the omnipresence, the song of a bird, the rustle of the leaves, the antics of a squirrel and even the slow, silent thrust of growing life. Was it not all speaking a language mysterious and divine? One must know how to listen and to understand without rejecting anything or disturbing anything, but humbly and with the greatest respect establish silence within oneself.

Through the pines, the breeze whispered gently. It hummed a lovely tune and Francis listened to the breeze speaking to him. Truly, the wind had become a fast friend. Was it not, as he was, a pilgrim and a stranger in this world, without a roof, ever wandering—always vanishing? The poorest among the poor, was it not carrying in its nakedness the priceless seeds of creation? It kept nothing for itself; it would sow and then move on without worrying where the seed would fall, without knowing anything about the fruit of its labor. It was content merely to sow and did it lavishly. Attached to nothing, it was as free as space itself. Wherever it wished, it whispered to the image of the Holy Spirit, as it is written in Scripture.

And while Francis listened to the song of the wind, it magnified his desire to share in the spirit of the Lord and God's sacred activity. This desire, as it suffused his soul, filled him with an immense peace. All the yearnings of his being were eased as they merged into this supreme desire.

One evening, returning from his tour of begging, Brother Sylvester told Francis about a farm where he had stopped and where he had lingered to console a poor mother whose baby was gravely ill. The infant could no longer retain any nourishment and vomited almost all that was eaten. The baby was wasting away and the mother was distraught at seeing her little one wilt from day to day without being able to do anything to save the child. It was heartbreaking. Just two years before, she had lost another child with a similar condition.* She was

---

* Probably pyloric stenosis, if one is permitted to diagnose seven centuries later.

discouraged and weeping, pitiful to see.

"I shall go and visit this poor woman," said Francis simply.

On the following morning, he set out alone across the woods and fields. The small farm was part of a hamlet and easy to recognize—"a low roof with thatched sides, the poorest and most miserable of all," Brother Sylvester had said.

In the small courtyard flooded with sunshine, a starving dog welcomed Francis. The animal ran to him, yelping and only stopped when it stuck its wet muzzle into his hand. The door of the house was ajar. Francis crossed the threshold, giving his usual salutation, the one that the Lord had taught him, "Peace to this house."

The silhouette of a woman appeared in the darkness and came toward the entrance. As soon as he could discern her facial expression, Francis had no difficulty in recognizing the mother of a sick child. The look about her, although still youthful, was so desolate and weary that it left no room for doubt.

"I have learned from Brother Sylvester," said Francis, "that you have a sick child and I have come to see the baby."

"You are Brother Francis, no doubt," said the woman, whose expression suddenly relaxed. "Brother Sylvester told me about you. Welcome, Brother, please come in."

Without further ado, she led him to the other end of the room to the child's cradle. The infant's eyes were open, but there was not the least expression of life in the waxen face. Francis bent over the child tenderly and tried to make the babe smile by making faces. But the child did not respond and only watched Francis with large eyes which were deeply shadowed and sunken in their sockets.

"Will the good Lord take this baby away from me, too, Father?" asked the woman, sorrowfully. "It would be the second in two years. Oh, that is hard!"

Francis was silent. The sorrow of this mother was not foreign to him. He understood it better than anyone because for months, he himself had been tormented by the very same sorrow. He, too, knew what it was to love his children and to see them fade away day after day. That was why this woman's grief touched him and stirred him so deeply.

"Poor mother," he said, after a few moments of silence. "It is hard, very hard, but you must not lose your confidence. Lose everything else, but not confidence."

He was not speaking just with his lips, without believing, or simply because he had to say something. No, he spoke from the very depths of his being and this woman felt it keenly. No doubt she had already been told these same things, but not in this way. She had never been impressed as she was now. Here, the words sprang forth from a different depth. He must have suffered grievously himself and perhaps lost all in order to speak with such sincerity and such gravity. He must have passed beyond despair and rediscovered solid ground, the deep reality that does not crumble.

Near the cradle a window overlooked the little garden behind the house. One could see the grandfather sitting in the shade of an apple tree all in blossom and on his knee he was holding a small boy and telling him a story. Nearby, in the grass, a little girl was playing with a black kitten.

"Are those your two older children with their grandfather?" Francis asked gently.

"Yes, they are my two older ones," answered the mother.

"They seem to be in good health," remarked Francis.

"Yes," she said with a bit of a pout. "Their health is fairly good. I haven't too much to complain about there, thank God."

"Yes, thank God," Francis agreed. "You are right in thanking God."

"It is true," observed the woman. "But if I had ten such as those, all healthy and lively, all of them could not replace the one I have lost. A child can never be replaced; it is always a unique being. When one of them disappears, all the others, however numerous, can never fill the void. The more a mother suffers for a little one, the dearer the babe is to her."

There was a moment of silence. In the stubble of the thatched roof a mouse was scurrying along with tiny steps. Outside in the small garden, the grandfather was continuing his story. One would think that he had come to the climax of the tale for his voice grew more grave and mysterious, while his face assumed a dramatic expression.

The little girl suddenly abandoned her kitten. She ran to her grandfather and in a coaxing voice was pleading with him, "Begin again, Grandfather, begin again. I didn't hear the first part."

"Let Grandfather tell it," retorted her brother, shoving her back with his arm.

The grandfather, pretending to hear nothing, continued his story with the greatest calm.

In the cradle the little one lay with closed eyes. Raising his hand, Francis blessed the baby and then quietly withdrew.

"Let the child sleep," he said to the mother. "I shall return soon to see the baby."

"My husband is in the fields right now," said the woman. "He will not be back until dusk, but surely you will say 'good day' to Grandfather before you go."

"No, leave him alone, please do," said Francis. "We must not disturb him now. That would spoil the children's pleasure. They need to hear their grandfather's stories. A childhood without stories is a morning without sunshine; it is a young plant without roots.

"I always remember the stories my mother told us when we were children. Our mother was from Provence and she knew the legends of France so well. On long winter evenings before going to sleep, we would snuggle up to her and with joy, sometimes mixed with fear, hear the marvelous tales of the Forest of Broceliande where Merlin the Enchanter lived as did the fairy Viviane. Another time she might tell us of the Emperor Charlemagne with his flowing beard or of his fearless knights Roland and Oliver. In our imaginations we could see the beautiful and gentle countryside with the Emperor Charlemagne riding by, escorted by his paladins.

"All of these memories linger and I feel they have become part of me; they sing in my heart. God speaks, too, in these humble voices of the earth. We must not scorn them. In fact, we must despise nothing, not even the fairy-queens, for they are the daughters of God."

The woman was listening to Francis, her gaze fixed on his face, so grave yet so gentle. The thing that struck her most was the immense goodness which was shining through his words, which radiated from all his being and extended to all things. While she looked at him and listened, the world assumed a new meaning, a new dimension. It became wide and deep, overflowing with hidden harmony. Nothing was superfluous; everything was intermingled in the same fundamental goodness. One could be safe anywhere because God was everywhere, even in the magical fables and fairy tales.

"You must come back to see us some evening," said the woman.

"I shall come very soon," said Francis, "but now I

must say good-bye."

Off he went through the woods and the fields. The sorrow of this poor mother weighed heavily on his heart. When he arrived at the hermitage he prayed for a long time in the twilight as was his custom.

This evening, however, his thoughts returned to the poor people he had visited and he asked the Lord not to lessen their poverty but to give them joy with poverty. For where there is joy mixed with poverty, there is neither greed nor avarice. He recalled the poor woman, so weary and discouraged, obviously waiting for help from him. He thought of all the other mothers, so weary and desolate. The suffering of this world seemed to him as immense and bottomless as in the night.

10

One Cannot Keep
the Sun from Shining

I shall come very soon," Francis
had said to the woman. Just a few days later, in the late
afternoon, he set out with Brother Leo to see the sick
child. The idea had occurred to him to take the packet of
flower seeds which Sister Clare had given him when he
left San Damiano.

"I shall sow the seeds under the children's window,"
he said to himself, "and that will bring a little joy to their
hearts. When they see their poor little house in flower,
they will love it all the more. There is such a difference
when one has known flowers in childhood."

Francis was musing on these thoughts as he trudged
through the woods behind Leo. The two of them were

used to taking silent walks together in the wilds of nature. Soon they were running down the slopes of a ravine toward a torrent which roared at the bottom. The place was remote with a savage and pristine beauty. The water, flung against the rocks, bounded back all white and exultant with brief bursts of azure. Its spray brought great freshness which penetrated the adjacent under-brush. A few junipers which had grown up here and there between the rocks were overhanging the bubbling water.

"Our sister water!" exclaimed Francis as he drew near the raging current. "Your purity sings of the innocence of God."

Leaping from one rock to another, Leo soon crossed the torrent. Francis followed but more slowly. Leo waited for him, standing on the far bank and watching the limpid water run rapidly over the golden sand between the gray masses of rock. When Francis caught up with him, Leo stood there in a contemplative mood. He seemed unable to detach himself from this scene and as Francis studied him he saw something of sadness in his expression.

"You are pensive," Francis commented simply.

"Oh, if we only had some of this purity," responded Leo, "then we, too, would know the mad, overflowing joy of our sister water and her irresistible enthusiasm."

Leo instilled into these words a deep melancholy. His wistful gaze was fixed on the swiftly moving stream which continued to flow in all its elusive purity.

"Come," Francis said to him, taking him by the arm.

And the two resumed their walk. After a moment of silence, Francis asked Leo, "Brother, do you know what purity of heart is?"

"It is to have no fault with which to reproach oneself," answered Leo without hesitation.

"Then I understand your sadness," said Francis, "because one always has something to regret."

"Yes," said Leo, "and that is precisely why I despair of ever achieving purity of heart."

"Oh, Brother Leo, believe me, you should not be so preoccupied with the purity of your soul," Francis replied. "Turn your gaze toward God. Marvel over God. Rejoice that God, at least, is all holy. Be grateful to God because of the Lord. That, little Brother, is the meaning of a pure heart.

"When you are thus focused on God, do not glance back at yourself. Do not ask yourself where you stand with God. Can't you see that the sadness of not being perfect and of discovering yourself a sinner is still a human sentiment—much too human?

"You must lift your gaze higher, ever so much higher. There is God, the immensity of God and the Lord's unutterable splendor. The pure heart never ceases to adore the true and living God. It takes a profound interest in the existence of God and, even in the midst of misery, is able to vibrate to the eternal innocence and joy of God. Such a heart is, at the same time, naked and gratified. For such a heart it is enough that God is God and in that it finds all its peace, all its pleasure. The Lord God becomes its holiness."

"However, God demands our effort and our faithfulness," observed Leo.

"Yes, without doubt," answered Francis, "but sanctity is not developing oneself to the utmost, nor is it an achievement of one's own doing. It is at first a void which one discovers in oneself and accepts and which God then comes to fill in proportion to how much one makes oneself receptive to God's bounty.

"Our nothingness, you see, if it is accepted, becomes a free space where God can create again. The Lord does not permit God's glory to be snatched by anyone. God is the Lord, the Only One, the Holy One. God takes the poor by the hand, pulling them from the mud, making them sit among the royalty of God's people so that at last they may see God's glory. God then becomes the azure atmosphere of the soul of the poor.

"To contemplate the glory of God, Brother Leo, to discover that God is God, eternally God beyond all we are or could ever be, to rejoice fully in what God is, to become ecstatic before God's eternal youth and to render God thanks because of God's being, because of God's inexhaustible mercy—that, Brother Leo, is the deepest obligation of this love which the spirit of God never ceases to infuse into our hearts. That is what it means to have a pure heart.

"This purity is not achieved by brute force or by becoming tense about it."

"Then how is it achieved?" demanded Leo.

"We must simply lose ourselves completely, sweep away everything, even the sharp perception of our distress. We must make room for God. We must accept poverty. We must renounce all that weighs us down, even the weight of our own faults. We must see nothing but the glory of God and bask in it. God is. That suffices. The heart then becomes buoyant. It no longer feels its own weight, but is like the lark, inebriated by space and sky. Then a person has abandoned all care, all worry. One's desire for perfection has changed into a simple and pure will for God."

Leo listened gravely as he walked on in front of his Father. And gradually, as he went along, he felt his own heart lift as a great peace spread over him.

They soon arrived in view of the small farm. Scarcely had they entered the front yard when they were hailed by the wife. Standing at the threshold of her home she seemed to be waiting for them and as soon as she saw them, she came to meet them. She was radiant.

"Oh, my brother," she said, addressing Francis in an excited voice, "I was indeed thinking that you would come this evening. I was anticipating your visit. If you only knew how happy I am! My little one is ever so much better and has been able to take some nourishment these past few days. I do not know how to thank you."

"God be praised!" exclaimed Francis. "It is God who is to be thanked."

Followed by Leo, he entered the low hovel and drawing near the cradle, leaned over toward the infant. He received a big, beautiful smile. The mother was completely exhilarated. Indeed, it was plain to see that the child had recaptured life.

Thereupon, the grandfather entered the house with the two older children running between his legs. He was a spry old man with a tranquil countenance and a peaceful, clear look in his eyes.

"Good evening, brothers," he said to them. "How kind of you to come to see us! We were really worried over the little one, but everything seems to have turned out well."

"I am so happy and I thank the Lord," said Francis.

"Oh, we ought to thank the Lord all the time," replied the old man calmly and gravely, "even when things do not turn out as we would have them. But then it is so difficult. We always lack hope.

"When I was young, I would sometimes demand an accounting from God when things were not going as I had wished. If God turned a deaf ear, I was flustered; I was even irritated. Now, I no longer demand the least accounting from God—that was something childish and ridiculous. God is like the sun. Whether one sees God or not, whether God appears or hides, God shines. Try to forbid the sun to shine! Well, we might as well try to keep God from pouring forth mercy."

"That is certainly true," said Francis. "God is goodness and God can only wish goodness. But unlike the sun which shines without us and above our heads, God has willed that the Lord's goodness pass through the hearts of people. Therein lies something wondrous and awesome. It depends on each of us, for our own part, whether or not other people will experience the mercy of God. That is why being good is so great a thing."

The two children who were leaning against their grandfather's legs gazed up at Francis and Leo with wide eyes filled with astonishment and a certain expectation. They were listening, or rather they were watching which was their way of listening. The look about Francis and his manner of speaking impressed them very much. Such vitality and sweetness emanated from him that they were completely spellbound.

"Well, then, let us be joyful," exclaimed Francis suddenly. "The little babe is better; we must rejoice!"

Then, he addressed the oldest child, whose eyes had not left him, "Come, my little one, I am going to show you something."

He took the child by the hand and drew him toward the front yard. Everyone followed, and the little girl was not the last one to run out and see what was going to happen.

"I have brought some flower seeds," said Francis, showing the packet to the child. "They are from very beautiful flowers. Where shall we sow them?"

Francis glanced around the yard. There, at the base of the wall under the windows, was a very old stone trough, which was fairly long and had been used for watering the animals in days gone by. It was full of earth and dead leaves and even weeds were sprouting there.

"The trough should serve the purpose very well," said the grandfather.

Francis immediately pulled out some of the weeds, loosened the soil and began to scatter the little seeds. Everyone watching him followed his hand as it moved quickly to and fro. They could barely catch sight of the tiny seeds as they fell.

"Why do you do that?" asked the little boy, intrigued.

"Because," answered Francis while continuing to sow, "when you see the little flowers open out to the sunshine and laugh in all their brilliancy, you will laugh too and you will say, 'How beautiful are the things the good God has made!' "

"And what are these little flowers called?" the little boy asked further.

"Oh, that I do not know," answered Francis. "But if you wish, we could call them *Speranza*.* Will you remember that name? They are the flowers of hope."

And the little boy, full of wonder, repeated distinctly: "*Spe-ran-za*."

---

* Italian for "hope."

At that moment, the father returned from his work. Stocky, dressed in an ashen tunic, his bare legs gray with dust, his face sunburned, his collar opened, his sleeves rolled up leaving his strong bronze arms exposed, he came toward the brothers with a broad smile which radiated the sunshine of the day.

"Good evening, brothers," he exclaimed. "It was a good idea to come this evening, for by good fortune I have finished my work a bit earlier. Ah! You have seen that the little one is very much better, isn't it so? It is truly extraordinary."

The general effect of the farmer's appearance expressed at the same time strength and simplicity. Fatigue in no way detracted from this expression of strong calm. On the contrary, it seemed to give him greater force.

"You will stay to sup with us," he said to the brothers in a friendly but decided way. Then he added, stepping back: "Excuse me for a moment while I wash up a bit. I shall be right with you."

He returned soon after, his face refreshed and he invited his guests to enter for supper. It was most simple, a thick soup and a few vegetables—the fare of the poor such as Francis loved.

After supper, they all withdrew to the small garden behind the house. The heat of the day had passed. The sun had disappeared behind the horizon, but its glow persisted still. Beyond, on the hill, on the side of the setting sun, some tall black cypress trees stood against the red and gold of the heavens, their huge tapered shadows stretching out over the fields. It was pleasant and calm as the entire family sat down on the grass under the apple tree. Their gaze was fixed on Francis.

After a moment of silence and expectation, the father of the family began the conversation, "My wife and I have for some time asked ourselves what we might do to live in a more perfect way. Of course, we cannot leave our children and lead the life of the friars. But what can we do?"

"It is enough for you to observe the Holy Gospel in the state to which the Lord has called you," answered Francis simply.

"But how are we going to put that into practice?" asked the father.

"In the Gospel," answered Francis, "the Lord tells you, for instance, to 'Let the greatest among you become as the least and the head as the one who serves.' Well, this counsel applies to every community including the family. Thus, the head of the family who must be obeyed and who is considered the greatest, ought to behave like the least and be the servant of all others. The head should thus take care of them with as much kindness as one would like to see shown if one were in their place.

"There should be sweetness and mercy in one's consideration for all. Faced with faults in any of them, one should not be irritated, but in all patience and humility should caution and support the errant one with gentleness. That is what it means to live according to the Holy Gospel. The one who acts that way has a true part in the spirit of the Lord. You need not dream of great things, but always return to the simplicity of the Gospel. More than anything else—take seriously this simplicity.

"Another example," continued Francis, "is when the Lord said, 'Blessed are the poor is spirit, for theirs is the Kingdom of Heaven.' Well, what is it to be poor in spirit? There are many who are perpetually at prayer or at office and repeatedly subject their body to abstinences and mortifications, but when a single word seems an affront or a trifle is taken from them, they are scandalized and in turmoil. They are not poor in spirit, for those whose spirit is truly poor hate themselves and cherish those who strike them on the cheek.

"One could multiply these examples and applications. Besides, in the Gospel everything is connected. You may begin at whichever end you like. You cannot truly possess one evangelical virtue without possessing all the others, nor can you offend one of them without offending all of them and thereby losing all.

"It is not possible to be truly poor according to the Gospel without being truly humble. And no one is truly humble who is not submissive to all creatures, but first and above all, to our sacred community, the church. This is an impossible task without great confidence in the Lord Jesus who never abandons his own and in the

Father who knows all our needs. The spirit of the Lord is one. It is a spirit of childhood, peace, mercy and joy."

Francis spoke even longer on this theme. For these farm people, guileless and open-hearted, it was a true joy to listen to him. But night was beginning to fall. It was clinging to the gnarled and somber branches of the apple tree. The two older children were nestled against their grandfather, from time to time giggling and indulging in some innocent joke. They were beginning to grow restless and fidgety. Francis and Leo thought it was then time to return home. They arose and took leave of their hosts.

It was pleasant to walk in the cool of the evening. The sky had become deep indigo and the stars were appearing one by one. Francis and Leo soon entered the forest. The moon had risen and its brightness touched the tops of the trees, slipping along the branches into the leaves until in the underbrush the light scattered into large drops of silver over the ferns and myrtle. There was a glow everywhere in the forest, a green light, soft and welcoming, which illuminated the distant recess of the immense corridors. In the trunks of the old trees, the lichen and moss were shining like stardust.

It seemed to Leo that this evening all the forest was awaiting someone. So beautiful was it with its interplay of lights and shadow, so elegant with the fragrance from the barks of the trees, from the ferns and mint and the myriad invisible flowers.

They walked in silence. In front of them a fox jumped

out of its hole and leaped into a pool of light, its red coat flaming for an instant. It soon disappeared into the shadows, howling faintly. A secret life was awaking. The night birds were calling to one another and innumerable murmurs came from the thick underbrush. In a clearing, Francis stopped and looked up at the sky. By now it was teeming with stars, all in clusters. They, too, seemed to be alive. The night was wonderfully clear and sweet. Francis breathed deeply and he found the forest fragrant.

All this invisible life, deep and quivering, which surrounded him, was not a dark and disquieting power. In his eyes it had lost its formidable character and its opacity. It had become light and by its very transparency, it revealed to him the Divine Goodness which is the source of all things. Then, resuming his walk with joyous step, he began to sing. The sweetness of God had seized him, the great and mighty sweetness of God.

"You alone are good. You are goodness itself, all goodness. You are our great sweetness. You are our eternal life, mighty and wondrous Lord," he repeated.

He was singing this with improvised melodies. In his joy, he picked up two pieces of wood and placing one over his left arm, he rubbed it with the other as if he were playing a violin. Leo was watching him. Francis' expression was radiant. He was walking and singing while mimicking the accompaniment of his song. Leo found it hard to keep up with him.

Suddenly Francis slowed his step and Leo saw,

stupefied, that the face of his Father had changed. It had become saddened—appallingly sad. He continued to sing, but even his song was sorrowful.

"Oh, You who have deigned to die for love of my love," he groaned, "let me know the sweet violence of your love that I may die for love of your love."

Leo was certain that at that moment Francis was seeing his Lord hanging from the ignominious cross. He was watching him after the long hours of agony, writhing still, struggling between life and death, a horribly tortured form. By one bound, his joy had transported him to a contemplation of the Crucified. The poor sticks dropped from his hands. Then he resumed his litany of praises in a stronger voice which resounded clearly in the night through all the forest.

"You are goodness, all goodness, great and adorable Lord, merciful Savior."

This rebound into joy surprised Leo. The image of the Crucified had not destroyed the joy of Francis. Quite the contrary. And Leo thought that it no doubt was the actual source of his joy, a source most pure and inexhaustible. This image of misery and opprobrium was the light which illuminated his path, it was that which revealed creation to him, which made him see God's creation beyond all the villainies and crimes of this world, a creation reconciled and filled with the sovereign goodness who is at the source of all things.

The face of Francis was wondrously illuminated anew

with the expression of a child, as if creation had just burst forth suddenly under his eyes, streaming with the innocence of God: the miracle of existence in its pristine freshness.

They crossed a clearing. At the edge of the woods, a herd of deer which were resting there got up. Motionless, their heads held high, the beasts were watching this person go by, this strange free person who was singing. They did not seem in the least afraid.

Then Leo realized he was witnessing an extraordinary moment. Yet, it was true indeed that the forest was waiting for someone this evening. All the trees and the animals, even the stars, were waiting for the passage of their human brother. No doubt nature had waited a long time—perhaps for thousands of years. But this evening, by a mysterious instinct, it knew that he was to come. And there he was in their midst, setting nature free with his song.

11

Poorer Than the Dead Wood

A thin column of bluish smoke was rising at the edge of the forest not far from the hermitage. It climbed, light and straight, undisturbed by the slightest breeze. Calm and tapering as a tall tree, it seemed to be part of the landscape.

It intrigued Brother Leo. The smoke was unusual. Who on earth had to light a fire this early in the morning? Leo wanted to know the whole story. He made his way, brushing aside the branches of a few shrubs and there, a stone's throw away, was Francis himself standing next to a meager fire. What, indeed, could he be burning? Leo saw him bend down to pick up a pine cone and throw it into the fire.

Leo hesitated an instant. Then he approached softly.

"What are you burning there, Father?" he asked.

"A basket," answered Francis simply.

Leo looked more closely. He distinguished the remains of a wicker basket which was almost destroyed by the fire.

"Isn't that the basket you have been making these past few days?"

"Yes, the very same," answered Francis.

"Why are you burning it? Were you not successful with it?" asked Leo, astonished.

"Oh, yes, very successful. Too successful, even," replied Francis.

"Brother, why are you burning it?"

"Because when we were reciting Terce just now, it distracted me to the point of monopolizing all my attention. It is justice that in return I should sacrifice it to the Lord," explained Francis.

Leo stood gaping at him. However well he knew Francis, his reactions were always surprising. This time his gesture appeared to Leo as an excessive severity.

"Father, I do not understand you. If we must burn all that distracts us in prayer, we would never be finished," murmured Leo after a moment of silence.

Francis made no reply.

"You know," added Leo, "Brother Sylvester was counting on this basket. He needed it and was waiting for it impatiently."

"Yes, I know. I will make another for him without delay. But I had to burn this one—it was even more urgent."

The basket was now completely burned and Francis smothered the fire under a stone. Taking Leo by the arm, he said:

"Come. I shall tell you why I acted this way."

He led him a short distance away, near a hedge of reeds. There he cut a sufficient number of flexible stems, sat down on the ground and began a new basket. Leo, sitting by his side, awaited the explanation from his Father.

"I want to work with my hands and I want all my brothers to work with their hands, too," declared Francis, "not for the greedy desire of earning money, but for the good example and in order to shun idleness. Nothing is more lamentable than a community where everyone does not work. However, work is not all, Brother Leo. It does not resolve everything. It could even become a formidable obstacle should persons permit themselves to be so engrossed by their work that they forget to adore the living and true God. That is why we must zealously see to it that nothing extinguishes the spirit of prayer within us. That is more important than anything."

"I understand that, Father," said Leo, "but in spite of all, we cannot really destroy our work each time it distracts us at prayer."

"Of course not," agreed Francis. "The important thing is to be ready to make the sacrifice to the Lord. Only on this condition are people able to keep their souls available to God. Under the ancient law, people sacrificed the firstfruits of their harvests and herds, offering them to God. They did not hesitate to deprive themselves of their finest. It was not only a gesture of adoration, but of liberation, too. They were keeping their souls open and the fact that they sacrificed broadened their horizon to the infinite. It was the secret of their freedom and of their greatness."

Francis became silent. All his attention seemed to focus on his work, but Leo, sitting beside him, could see that he still had something to say, something that was an essential part of him but which he was finding difficult to express. Leo felt certain about this. Hence, the minutes of silence seemed endless. He longed to say something, to ease the silence, but restrained himself discreetly.

Suddenly Francis turned toward him with an expression of loving kindness. "Yes, Brother Leo," he said with grave calm, "people are not great until they rise above their work to see God alone. It is only then that they reach their full stature. But that is difficult to do—so very difficult. To burn a wicker basket of one's own making— that is nothing at all, even when the basket is perfectly made. However, to divorce oneself from the work of an entire lifetime, that is something else, something above human strength.

"To follow the call of God, people give themselves completely to a project, enthusiastically, passionately.

That is good, even necessary, for such enthusiasm is creative. However, to create something is to put one's mark on it, to declare it one's own irrefutably. The servant of God then runs the greater danger. One's creation, insofar as one has become attached to it, becomes the center of one's universe and puts one in a state of fundamental entanglement. There must be a deliberate disruption to free someone from it.

"Thank God, this disruption does occur; but the providential means which are then set to work are formidable, indeed. They are lack of understanding, contradiction, suffering, failure and sometimes even sin itself which God permits. The life of faith then experiences its most profound and decisive crisis. Such a crisis is inevitable and sooner or later presents itself in all walks of life.

"Those who have dedicated themselves to their work without reservation have believed that they were giving glory to God through their generosity. Suddenly God seems to desert them, to lose interest in what they are doing. Even worse, God seems to ask them to renounce their work and abandon everything to which they have devoted their body and their soul through so many years of joy and suffering.

" 'Take your son, your only one, the one you love and go into the country of Moria—and there offer him as a sacrifice.' This terrible command was spoken by God to Abraham. There are no true servants of God who do not hear it themselves when their own turn comes. Abraham believed in God's promise to give him offspring and for 20 years awaited its realization. He did not despair. When, at long last, the child had come, the child on whom the promise rested, God summoned Abraham to sacrifice him, without the least explanation. It was a ruthless and incomprehensible blow.

"Well, it is the very same thing that God will also demand of us some day. Then God and humans no longer seem to speak the same language. A misunderstanding has occurred. God had called and a person had responded, but now, this same person calls and God remains silent. This is the tragic moment when the religious life borders on despair, when a person struggles all alone in the night with the intangible. A person believed that it would be sufficient to do this or that in order to be pleasing to God. But now everything is turned against them.

"People are not saved by works, however good they may be, but rather, they themselves have to become the work of God. They must make themselves more formless and malleable in the hands of their Creator than clay is in the hands of the potter. They must be more supple and more pliable than rush in the fingers of the basket weaver. They must be more desolate and abandoned than the dead wood of the forest in the heart of winter. Only by starting from this pitiful condition and avowing complete poverty of spirit can people offer a boundless trust to God, confiding to God the absolute initiative of their existence and of their salvation. They then embrace a holy obedience and become a child playing the divine game of creation. Beyond pain and gratification, they come to discover joy and power. They can fathom to equal depths sunshine and death, with the same gravity and the same lightheartedness."

Leo was silent. He no longer desired to pose any questions. He certainly did not understand all that Francis had said, but never before had he seen so clearly and so deeply into the soul of his Father. What impressed Leo more than anything else was the serenity with which Francis discussed these grave things which he must know by experience.

Leo remembered that at another time Francis had told him: "Someone only knows for certain what one has experienced." Surely he had experienced all that he had just said. It had such a ring of truth. Leo was suddenly filled with sweetness and awe at the thought of being the privileged confidant of such an experience.

Francis himself continued his work and his hand twisted the reeds without trembling, as if there were nothing to it.

12

Sunnier Than Summertime

The crickets were singing in the pine grove around the hermitage. It was early June and extremely warm. The unrelenting sun was flaming in the dazzling blue of the sky. Its rays, straight and dense, were falling like a rain of fire. Nothing escaped this conflagration. In the forest, the bark of the trees was cracking under the drying effects of the heat. On the steep slopes of the mountain, the dried and yellowed grass was scorched between the rocks. At the edge of the woods, the shrubs and young green plants, still distended by the spring rains, lowered their heads sadly. However, near the little oratory, several apple trees, with young fruit amid their leaves, seemed to bear up and be quite comfortable in the blistering heat. The searing sun like a purging fire was putting every living thing to the test.

It forced every being to reveal its true self. Nothing immature could withstand it—only the fully grown could. Only the tree that had begun to develop sound fruit could offer itself without fear to the brilliance and dazzle of the devastating sun.

In the very warm hours of the day, Francis liked to meditate under the pines. He listened to the crickets and inwardly joined in their incessant chirping. Although his eyes were always troublesome, his heart was at peace. In the heat of midday, he could always feel something of the tranquility of evening. No doubt the thought of the meeting of the order at Pentecost, just a few days away, must have crossed his mind. He thought of the multitude of brothers whom he was going to see on this occasion at Assisi. He could envision the difficulties which would not fail to crop up again in the heart of his large family, difficulties more forceful and formidable than ever. He reflected on these things, unruffled, for they no longer oppressed him. Even the painful memories that such a thought inevitably recalled could not disturb the serenity of his soul. Not that he had become indifferent! Oh, no—his love for his own and his demands on them had never ceased to grow and deepen. But he was at peace. For him, too, the hour of maturity had come. He was not anxious to know whether he would bear much fruit. But he was solicitous lest his fruit be bitter. This was the only thing that mattered. He knew that all "these things would be given to him besides." Above him, the crickets did not stop their chirping. Their shrill notes had the crackle of fire as they fell from the high branches like flaming tongues.

Francis was sitting in the pine grove when he saw a tall, slender friar coming to him through the woods: the brother, still young, had a slow, deliberate step. Francis recognized Brother Tancred and, arising, he hurried to meet him and embrace him.

"Peace to you!" said Francis. "What a pleasant surprise! You must be warm from climbing all the way up here."

"Oh, yes, Father," answered the brother as he wiped his brow and then the rest of his face with his sleeve. "But that is nothing." The brother shook his head and gave a sigh. Francis invited him to sit down in the shade of the pines.

"What is the matter? Tell me," said Francis.

"You know the story well, Father," said Tancred. "Since the day you ceased to be among us as our head, everything has been crumbling. The friars—and I refer to those who wish to remain faithful to the Rule and to your example—those friars are discouraged and they have lost their bearings. They are told repeatedly that you have been superseded and they must adjust themselves, that they must draw inspiration from the organization of the other great orders and must produce great scholars who can rival those of other orders. They are told that simplicity and poverty are very beautiful things but should not be exaggerated and at any rate, they are not enough. Science, power and money are also indispensable for achieving results. That is what they are told."

"No doubt the same ones are saying these things," observed Francis, simply. "The ones who always do."

"Yes, Father, the same ones. You know them. They are called the innovators, but they have seduced many. And the tragedy of it all is that by reacting against them, certain friars go to all sorts of eccentricities, in the worst taste, under the pretext of austerity and evangelical simplicity. The friars who thus pretend were reprimanded very recently by the bishop of Fondi because they were neglecting themselves completely and growing beards of absurd length. Others have broken their vows and taken wives. They don't seem to realize that by acting this way they bring discredit on all the community and throw fuel on the fire of the innovators. With their abuses, the eccentric friars have played into the hands of the innovators, who now are posing as defenders of the Rule in order to impose their will. Caught between the innovators and the eccentrics, there are the faithful few who bleat because they are without a shepherd. It is truly a pity. And now, the meeting of the chapter at Pentecost approaches! It is our last hope. Will you go to Assisi, Father?"

"Yes, I will go and I think I shall set out without delay," answered Francis simply.

"The faithful friars hope that you are going to take up

the governing powers once more and that you will curb
the abuses and squelch the recalcitrants. It is high time!"

"Do you think that the others want me?" inquired
Francis.

"You must impose yourself, Father, by speaking in a
loud and forceful voice and by threatening sanctions. You
must resist them directly. It is the only way," retorted
Tancred.

Francis did not answer. The crickets were singing. At
times, the forest sighed. A light breeze stirred the pine
grove, wafting a strong fragrance of balsam. Francis was
silent, staring at the ground strewn with needles and dry
twigs. He was struck by the thought that any chance
spark thrown on this carpet would be enough to enkindle
the entire forest.

"Listen," said Francis after several moments of
silence, "I do not want to leave you with an illusion. I
will speak plainly to you since that is what you wish. I
would not consider myself a Friar Minor if I were not in
the state I am in here. I am the superior of my brothers.
I shall attend the chapter, preach a sermon and give my
opinion. And when I have finished, they will tell me, 'You
do not have what is needed; you are illiterate and
despicable. We no longer want you as a superior because
you are not the least bit eloquent. You are simple-minded
and limited.' Then I shall be banished shamefully,
inundated by universal contempt. Well, I tell you, if I
could not take that with the same aplomb, with the same

carefree heart, maintaining a steady course toward sanctification, I would not be—no, not in the least—a Friar Minor."

"That is very fine, all of it—but it does not resolve the question," objected Tancred.

"What question?" asked Francis.

Tancred looked at him, dumbfounded.

"What question?" repeated Francis.

"That of the order, of course!" exclaimed Tancred. "You have just described your state of soul for me. I admire it, but you cannot stop at this personal viewpoint and dream only of your perfection. There are others. You are their guide and their Father. You cannot abandon them. They have a right to your support. You must not forget them."

"That is true, Tancred. There are the others and I do think of them, believe me," said Francis. "However, one cannot help others to practice meekness and evangelical patience by starting to pummel all those who do not hold the same opinion, but rather by accepting the blows oneself."

"But the Word of God—what do you make of that?" retorted Tancred in a lively fashion. "There is a holy anger. Christ cracked the whip over the heads of the money changers—and not just over their heads, I am sure! Sometimes we must chase the money changers from the temple even if it means material loss and disturbance. That, too, is to imitate Christ."

Tancred had raised his tone. He was animated, speaking with fire, with abrupt gestures. His face was flushed. He made a motion to get up, but Francis placed a hand on his shoulder and held him.

"Wait, Brother Tancred, listen to me a bit," he said calmly. "If the Lord wished to banish out of sight all that is impure and unworthy, do you think there are many who would not be found wanting? We would all be swept away, my poor friend—we like the others. There is not such a difference among people from this point of view. Happily, God does not care to make a clean sweep. That saves us. True, Christ once threw the money changers out of the temple. He did it just to show us that he could—that it was his right for he is the Master of his house. But you will notice that Jesus did it only once and as if playing a game, after which, he surrendered himself to the blows of his prosecutors. By this, he shows us the patience of God—not an inability to be severe but a will to love—which he will never renounce."

"Yes, Father, but in acting as you say, you are defaulting at the game, purely and simply. The order will be lost and the church will suffer greatly because of it. Instead of a rejuvenation, it will number one more among the ruins. That is all," replied Tancred.

"Well, I tell you, the order will continue in spite of everything," affirmed Francis with vigor but without surrendering his calm. "The Lord has made it clear to me. The future of the order is God's affair. If the brothers are unfaithful, it will be resuscitated by others. Perhaps they have already been born. As for me, the Lord has not asked me to convince people by force of eloquence or knowledge and much less to constrain them. God has simply let me know that I ought to live according to the Holy Gospel. When the Lord gave me the brothers, I had a simple Rule written in a few words. The Holy Father has confirmed it for me. We were then unpretentious and submissive to all. I wish to persevere in that state until the end."

"Then we must let the others act as they please and endure everything without saying anything?" retorted Tancred.

"For me, I wish to be submissive to all people and to all creatures of the world—as much as Almighty God permits. That is what it means to be a Friar Minor."

"Not that truly, Father. I do not follow you, I do not understand you," said Tancred.

"You do not understand me," resumed Francis, "because this attitude of humility and submission seems to you like cowardice and passivity. But it is something very different. I, too, was without understanding for a long time. I struggled with myself in the night, like a poor bird caught in a trap. But the Lord took pity on me and made me see that the highest activity of persons and of their maturity does not rest in the pursuit of an idea, however lofty and holy it may be, but in the humble and joyous acceptance of whatever is—of all that is. Those who merely follow their own ideas remain locked within themselves. They do not truly commune with creation. They never become acquainted with the universe. They lack silence, depth and peace. The depth of anyone is in proportion to their receptive capacity. The greater part of humanity remains isolated within themselves, despite all appearances. They are like insects unable to shed their cocoons. They are desperately agitated in the dark reaches of their limitations. At the end of it all, they find themselves as they were when they started. They think they have changed something, but they die without ever having seen the day. They have never awakened to reality; they have lived in a dream."

Tancred was silent. These words of Francis seemed so strange. Was it he or Francis who was dreaming? It was irritating to see himself fall among the dreamers. He was sure of himself and of all that he was seeing and feeling.

"But then they are all dreamers, all those who try to accomplish something in this world," he said after a moment of silence.

"I did not say that," responded Francis. "But I do think that it is difficult to accept reality. And, to tell the truth, no one ever accepts it totally. In one way or another we are always trying 'to add one cubit to our height.' It is the root of most of our actions. In fact it is still that which we are often seeking when we think we are working for the Kingdom of God. Then one day we are jarred by failure, a profound failure, and the only thing left to us is this prodigious reality: God is.

"We then discover that God alone is all powerful. God alone is all God. The one who accepts this reality and rejoices in it from the heart has found peace. God is and that suffices. Only those who accept God in this way are capable of truly accepting themselves. They become free of all specific desires and for them nothing more will ever disturb the joyful harmony of creation. Their desires have become simplified and at the same time as vast and stupendous as the universe; they have been resolved into a simple and pure craving for God which embraces everything and welcomes anything.

"Nothing more separates them from the act of the Creator. They are entirely receptive to the workings of God which make them whatever God wishes and lead them wherever God wants. This holy obedience gives them access to the profundity of the universe, to the power which moves the stars and makes the humble flowers of the field burst forth so gloriously. They see clearly into the heart of the world.

"Humanity discovers the sovereign goodness which is the origin of all beings and which one day will be in all, but in the discovery sees this goodness even now spreading out and flowering in every creature. Then participating in the great framework of this goodness, people become merciful, radiating warmth just like the Father, who commands the sun to shine on the good and on the bad with equal extravagance.

"Oh, Brother Tancred, how great is the glory of God! The world is brimming over with God's beauty and God's mercy."

"But in the world there are also error and evil," retorted Tancred. "We cannot avoid them, and when we see them, we do not have the right to be indifferent. Woe to us, if by our silence or inertia the wicked become obdurate in their malice and eventually triumph."

"It is true, we cannot be indifferent in the face of evil or error," resumed Francis, "but we should be neither irritated nor dismayed by it. Such dismay and irritation will only restrict the charity within us or in others. Rather must we learn to see evil and error as God sees them. It is precisely that which is so difficult. Where we would tend to see an error to be condemned and to be punished, God sees, from the very start, a suffering to be alleviated.

"The All-Powerful One is at the same time the meekest of beings and the most patient. In God there is no trace of resentment. When we creatures rebel and offend God, we remain God's creatures still. God, of course, could destroy us, but what pleasure could God find in destroying something which was made with so much love? The roots of all God's creatures are ever deep within the Lord. God is the most disarmed of all beings when faced by those creatures loved into being, as a mother is before her child. There, my brother, is the secret of that stupendous patience which sometimes scandalizes us.

"God is like the parent of a family who sees the children grown up and eager to assert their independence and who says to them: 'You wish to leave; you are impatient to live your own life in your own way. Very well, but I wish to tell you this before you leave: if there comes a day when you are troubled and in distress, know that I am always here. My door shall ever be wide open, by night or day. You may always come. You will be at home and I will do everything I can to help you. When every door is closed to you, remember, my door will always be open.'

"God is that way, too, Brother Tancred. No one loves as God does. We must try to imitate God; until now we have done nothing, so let us get started."

"But at which end should we begin, Father? Give me one practical way. Which is the most urgent?" asked Tancred.

"The most urgent thing," answered Francis, "is to desire to possess the spirit of the Lord. God alone can make us good, fundamentally good, with a goodness which then becomes one with our deepest nature."

He was silent for a moment, then he resumed, "The Lord has sent us to evangelize the world. But have you already thought about what it means to evangelize people? Can't you see, Brother, that to evangelize a person is to say to that one: 'You—yes, you too are loved by God in the Lord Jesus.'

And you must not only tell that person so, but you must really believe it, and not only believe it, but conduct yourself with this person in such a way that this person can feel and discover there is something within that is being redeemed, something more majestic and noble than had ever been dreamed.

"Thus will this person be aroused to a new awareness of self. Thus will you have proclaimed to that one 'the good tidings of great joy.' This will be possible only if you offer that person your friendship, a true friendship, unbiased and without condescension, a friendship rooted in profound confidence and esteem.

"We must go unto all people, but that is not easy. The world of people is a huge battlefield for wealth and power, and too much suffering and atrocity can eclipse the face of God. In going to everyone we must above all never appear to them as a new species of competitor. We must stand in the midst of them as the peaceful witnesses for the All Powerful, as those who covet nothing and scorn no one, people capable of truly becoming their friends. It is our friendship that they are waiting for, a friendship that should make them feel they are loved by God and redeemed in Jesus Christ."

The sun slipped behind the mountains and suddenly the air was sweeter and cooler. The wind was stirring and nudged the trees. It was almost night now and from everywhere one could hear the steady crescendo of the uninterrupted chant of the crickets.

Additional copies of this book may be obtained
from your local bookstore
or by sending $10.95 per paperback copy, postpaid,
or $15.95 per hardback copy, postpaid, to:

Hope Publishing House
P.O. Box 60008
Pasadena, CA 91116

California residents please add 8.5% sales tax
FAX orders to (818) 792-2121
Telephone VISA/MC orders to (800) 326-2671